Anither Pot o' Broth

Also by Jack Cooper:

A POT OF ISLAND BROTH   The Orkney View 1988

JACK COOPER

Anither Pot o' Broth

COVER PAINTING BY THE AUTHOR

Full plate line drawings by Harald Nicolson

Tailpieces by Inga Nicholl

published by

THE ORKNEY VIEW

ISBN 1 870460 03 0

Published by:-
The Orkney View, 3 Papdale Close, Kirkwall, Orkney
Typesetting and layout by:-
The Orkney View, 3 Papdale Close, Kirkwall, Orkney
Printed by:-
The Orcadian Ltd., Victoria Street, Kirkwall, Orkney

To the Senior Citizens of the Islands

Introduction

When I offered "A Pot of Island Broth" a year ago, I did so with considerable trepidation, realizing that an old man's reminiscences might be a bit indigestible.

However, I am now able to express sincere gratitude to all the kind people in Orkney and beyond who, by their appreciation, have encouraged me to continue my untutored efforts.

The greater volume of praise has come from my contemporaries who seem to have no difficulty in digesting island broth, and it is to them that I offer this second helping, in the hope that in recording the life and times of a peedie boy of a generation fast disappearing something of that uncomplicated life style may yet permeate the hustle and bustle of the present time and bring to the reader a measure of the peace I have found in remembering them.

Again I offer sincere thanks to Alastair and Anne Cormack for their help and encouragement and to Harald Nicolson for his faithful and witty translation of my thoughts into lively illustrations.

To Dora I offer unstinted praise for her patience and constructive criticism, and for her gracious acceptance of the role of Orcadian by proxy.

Jack Cooper
Bluebell Hill
Kent
June 2 1989

Contents

The Enchanted Years

The shadowy recollection of a rusty steam capstan turning slowly; the coiling of an enormous rope; the calloused hand of a seaman gently moving me out of the way, and a smaller, softer hand leading me along a precarious gangway; a lady with bright eyes and a nice smile lifting me on to a bed of straw in a cart; those are the things that lie upon the threshold of the Enchanted Years. It was strange and disturbing, but because my 'mither' climbed into the cart together with the bright-eyed lady and drew me gently to her I knew it was all right. 'Mither' was Aunt Betty who had taken me into her home in Sanday, and had nursed me through whooping cough and given me all the love and care that would doubtless have been mine had my mother survived the fever that followed the birth of my sister.

My father, shattered by bereavement, decided to pursue his intention of emigrating to Canada, but now alone, leaving my infant sister in the care of my mother's sister in Glasgow. Whatever his intention, the family never came together again, save for a couple of brief interludes when he returned to Westray on holiday in later years. All this gradually impinged itself upon my mind, although by the time I became fully aware of my early misfortunes, I no longer felt any grief. Whatever the effect upon my subconscious mind, it made little impact upon my new life in Westray.

The bright-eyed lady in the cart with us was Daisy, the youngest of my four aunts, twenty-one or two and unmarried. She was kindness itself to me, and carried me indoors after a seemingly endless journey behind the slow plodding white horse, guided by a big bearded man with a stern face, who spoke little. Then another face swam into my consciousness - a face which seemed to be an amalgam of 'mither' and the bright-eyed lady, older, perhaps, but warm and kind and friendly - the face of my dear Grandmother. I can feel the warmth of her personality now. She lifted me and pressed me to her, tears streaming down her cheeks - tears for her bereaved eldest son, and her prematurely dead daughter-in-law whom she had not seen. Perhaps some of the tears were for me. Although they were beyond my understanding at the time I can share them with her now as I write.

But this was no time for tears! All was new and wonderful and a little mysterious. The peat fire was at the wrong end of the room, and the hearth was wider, and festooned with drying fish. The 'girnel' was larger too, and painted white, as was the dresser and the 'press'. The 'cupples' of the roof were covered by varnished boards so that they didn't show, and hams hung from hooks screwed into the boards. I felt a little apprehensive when the big stern man came in. He picked me up with large hands that smelt of harness and horses, and his face was so hairy! But his eyes were kind, as they twinkled and grew moist as he held me out at arm's length and inspected me. I cannot remember what he said because I was a little perturbed, and wished he would put me down, but I gather the gist of it was that although I had the face of a McDonald (my mother's name) I was Cooper-like aboot the eyes. If that be true (and I doubt it not) it spelled acceptance into the family.

Aunt Betty's husband and daughter Betty required her presence in Sanday, and she departed after a few days, and, although I was distraught at her going, the warmth of my welcome soon enabled me to transfer the title of 'mither' to Grandmother, and, as her natural consort, Grandfather became 'feyther' and we dwelt together as a family. I have since realized what a sacrifice it must have been for them both to start again with a young child when the youngest of their own family, Uncle Eddie, was nineteen.

Sleeping arrangements were a little uncertain at first. With mistaken kindness a little nest was arranged for me across the foot of my grandparents' bed, while I became used to my new surroundings. That suited me very well. I felt cosy and protected, although Grandfather's horny feet presented a constant hazard when he stretched his legs. But that was a privilege which could not last! Aunt Daisy volunteered to share her bed with me, and that was gladly accepted. I was fond of her, and she of me, but once again that happy state of affairs was sabotaged. I wet the bed! As every dog is entitled to one bite, so small boys are permitted one accident, but, unfortunately accidents recurred from time to time, due, no doubt, to some psychological disturbance, and I was transferred to the more austere location of the 'boy's end', where in former times my father and my uncles had fought and roistered and slept. There I shared a room, or 'end' with a miscellany of household goods and utensils, adjuncts of fishing, butter making, and all the paraphernalia of crofting life.

My bed was cosy enough with fresh straw, a chaff-filled mattress, called a 'bedseck' and plenty of warm homespun blankets, not forgetting a precautionary waterproof underblanket. But it was lonely at first. For a few nights the battle raged. At first my largely synthetic sobbing moved Grandmother to compassion, but after the third night the moment of truth arrived! My tears were ignored, and when I heard the 'ben end' door firmly closed from the exclusive side I capitulated, beaten. Even then, Grandmother's compassionate nature continued to soften the bitter blow. On her final visit to get me up for a pre-emptive drain off she contrived to introduce an affectionate old house cat to my bed. An immediate friendship sprang up, and for a long time I had a real live 'teddy' that purred whenever I stretched out a searching hand, and offered solace during the brief time between saying my 'Bonny Wirds' to 'The Good Man' and going to sleep.

On waking up of a summer morning I needed no other company than that which was built into the back of my box bed. It had been papered with samples from a book of nursery papers. There were sailing boats, birds, flowers, and a multiplicity of bright designs for the delectation of young minds, but my favourite was a panel depicting a group of children at play - immaculate children in sailor suits with spotless white collars, and girls in gleaming pinafores and straw hats with streaming ribbons. Petrified skipping ropes raised no dust, and well-behaved puppies kept their appointed places. I knew only two children's names, my own, Johnnie, and Betty, my cousin now left in Sanday, and lost to me for the time being. They were bestowed upon the biggest and brightest of the paper company. On the roof of the bed were drawn beautiful sailing ships, the work of my father and uncles. They too had names but as I couldn't read I had to be content with studying their tall masts and spidery rigging. At the head of the bed there was a wide crack between the boards, and in the early morning the sunshine streaming through promised a fine day, and the swimming motes of dust danced when I blew gently into the stream.

A knot hole in the back board allowed limited observation of the 'but end' so that I could watch Grandfather stirring the peat fire into life each morning, and hanging the porridge pot from the 'crook'. It was a simple routine, but one which spelled a kind of stability, as it presaged Grandmother's emergence from the 'ben end', and the beginning of another day. I was allowed to get up when she appeared. Grandfather disapproved of me getting 'under his feet' first thing in the morning. Each day promised fresh adventures and discoveries. Being summer, the byres and stables were empty and silent, except for the questing hens to whom every open door was an invitation. The live stock enjoyed their fill of lush grass and slept under the stars, their choice of bed limited only by the length of their tethers. Even the milking was carried out alfresco except when it was raining. It was a joy to sally forth, Grandmother carrying the 'creepie' while I struggled proudly with the enamelled pail, holding the handle chest high to keep the bottom off the ground, and walking warily lest I trip over one of the attendant convoy of cats who never missed the portion of steaming milk doled out when it was brought to the 'milk-hoose' to be strained, or 'syed' prior to being 'set' in shallow earthenware pans to allow the cream to rise. They received their portion in the broken bottom of an ancient three-toed pot, and lapped, five heads together, and five tails fanning out in a circle like a colourful flower.

My exploration of the empty byres produced a find when I discovered half a dozen eggs concealed in a wisp of straw in the corner of a stall. "Luk whit a'm fund," was my breathless announcement. Grandmother was pleased that the designs of some broody hen had been thwarted. Had nature taken its course, an unwanted and ill-timed brood would no doubt have emerged, and a dozen eggs would have been lost from the quota destined for the van. I was pronounced a good boy and promised one of the eggs for my tea. I would have had one anyway, but that was 'special'. I was well fed upon good plain wholesome food. Having thus distinguished myself, I assiduously searched the empty stalls each day, and occasionally carried an egg in triumph to be presented with as much pride as if I had laid it myself. One day I experienced the thrill of seeing a hen actually laying, which was one of my earliest introductions to the facts of life! I can hear now the paean of self-congratulation emanating from her as she rose to inspect and confirm her daily effort.

Gradually my fascinating explorations extended beyond the stone walls of the 'kailyard' until the stack yard and the many out-houses became familiar territory. They were by no means lonely sorties, because there were hens everywhere, clucking and 'talking' contentedly over their truly free range, or enjoying an exotic feast when Grandfather tipped a cartload of fresh shingle from the beach, teeming with all kinds of hoppers, 'sholties' and invertebrate foreshore life, and at the same time recharging their ever-active gizzards with grit. I learned the names of the buildings added haphazardly to the steading as necessity and progress demanded. There was the 'tattie-hoose', the 'big henny-hoose', the 'peedie henny-hoose', the 'burdie-hoose', the henny hoose 'abune the hoose'. And there was the sty, and the 'deukie-hoose', and 'Jeck's hoose', a lean to, or 'teu-fa' edifice reputedly built single-handed by my Uncle John in his boyhood. Grandmother told me how he had celebrated its completion by cooking a duff in it over an ill-ventilated peat fire and an improvised 'lum', and had been unable to eat his achievement for coughing. But its glory had long since departed, and now it housed the small stock of coal used to supplement the dwindling supply of peat available from the 'hill'.

During the first days (or was it weeks?) of this new phase of my life I sensed some vague gap in the scheme of things until I identified it as the absence of my erstwhile companion and 'minder', cousin Betty. She was far away in Sanday with her mother and father and I was told that Aunt Betty now had a 'bairn' called Mary Jane. This devastating piece of news finally seemed to exclude me from the Family at Newark. They seemed so far away - Da, Granny, 'mither', and 'feyther' whose dark smiling weatherbeaten face I only dimly remember. He was away on the farm all day, and I saw little of him.

There were children next door, at a house called Costie's, whom I had seen at play, but whom I had not met so far. No doubt they were self-sufficient and therefore did not seek my company, and I had not yet been encouraged to extend my explorations beyond the steading. However, when the time was deemed to be ripe, Grandmother took me over the ditch which separated the holdings and introduced me to Hughie, and Annie, and Rita. There were others, but they were older and totally disinterested in shrimp-sized strangers. First overtures were not encouraging. Hugh, a couple of years older than I, and already attending school, gave me a cool appraisal and summed me up with the remark, "Beuy, thoo're a funny like thing." Thus, whether intentionally or not, he established immediate supremacy, an advantage which he continued to enjoy during our school days. He was bigger and stronger than I, but we became firm friends and shared many escapades. About my own age was his youngest sister, Annie, and in the days before we started school we were like brother and sister. I need not dwell upon our happy liaison, as I have recorded it elsewhere, but we still recall the enchanted years whenever we meet.

And so, with youthful companionship established, my horizons continued to broaden. I shared in many of the activities of the Costie family. Together we roamed the fields, although Annie and I were regarded more as encumbrances than companions at first. We could not jump the deeper ditches or run fast enough. Each field was of necessity identified. Usually the location sufficed: there was 'the piece next tae Titherhoose', and 'next tae Cubbigeo' or 'below the hill', or 'ower the ditch', or 'back o' the hoose'. And there was the 'hill' itself, ten acres of peaty moorland covered with tussocks of heather and coarse grass, the haunt of redshanks and teewhuppos, as we called the lapwings which claimed it as their country and protested loudly when we invaded. In the season we searched and found the scrapes where they laid their olive eggs with dark spots, and marked each one with a little cairn of stones. After the nesting season we burned the heathery 'tuos' and laughed and shouted round the fires like young savages, and were happy. As we grew in stature, the inevitable day approached when Annie and I would achieve the ultimate translation to the Real World, the 'Schule'. It was with envy that we watched the 'big eens' striding importantly with their satchels, and heard their returning tales of weighty matters and grown-up events from playground and classroom.

Aunt Daisy, ever attentive to my needs, gave much time to preparing me for school. I already knew the alphabet, although not yet how to apply it. I learned readily under her tuition, and I loved and trusted her. I am sure she found pleasure in shaping my awakening intelligence, because she was a born teacher, and indeed was employed as such from time to time in those days when aptitude was rated higher than academic certificates. Only once did I rebel, quite mistakenly, against her kindness. It was harvest time, and with it a thick sea mist. Potatoes were being lifted because crops were too wet to cut, and, as usual I was busy getting in everyone's way, and becoming so engrossed that when it was time to go home in the gathering dusk, I had become so disorientated by the mist that when she made to lead me home I was convinced that I was being led in the wrong direction. When I protested she picked me up to carry me, but when the vague outline of the house loomed up I was more than ever convinced that I was being shanghaied into yet another strange place. It looked so high and different from a somewhat unusual angle that I laid down the law in no uncertain terms. "That's no wurrus," I declared. "If thoo taks me tae that hoose I'll keek thee ap the lum."

It was not until I was carried struggling indoors and beheld all the familiar things that I was finally mollified. The thought of Aunt Daisy being elevated up the chimney on my tiny toe caused much merriment!

All the bustle and business of 'hairst' filled many days with enchantment. The familiar fields took on a newer and larger dimension shorn of their waving rigs of oats and regimented by rows of stooks. Ditches which had disappeared became real landmarks once more. What excitement to watch the clattering reaper as it passed and to watch the next swathe of oats tremble before the knife and fall with a soft rustle on to the sheafboard. Then a deft movement of the rake and a bent knee slid another sheaf to the ground to be gathered, bound and stooked, and summer became autumn in one magical movement. A new enchantment manifested itself when the 'half-yoke' basket was brought. Tea and milk and bread and jam, and scones with currants, and perhaps a slice of cold duff, or a length of mealy pudding. Eating with one's back propped against a stook was surely the ultimate in enchantment - something to be enjoyed to the uttermost, especially when it was the turn of Branstane to have the reaper and the workers. Grandfather shared the reaper with his brother-in-law, Uncle Tom of Branstane, and they went all the way by pooling the resources of labour as well.

Once, when dusk had halted operations, and the horse was unharnessed from the reaper and the saddle removed, Uncle Tom set me upon the great steaming back of the horse and I was carried to the stable clinging desperately to the swaying mane. When I was lifted my little tail end felt all hot and damp; but I had ridden a real horse. Another giant step in my life! Those far-off days stamped me with a love of crofts and crofting and the whole and simple things of life, a love which has never left me although the greater part of my life has been channelled into disciplines far removed from the rig and the furrow.

The glamour of harvest faded before the short days

and the long dark nights of winter when the hatch in the ceiling above my bed rattled when the wind blew, and the morning sun never reached the crack in my bed. Sometimes I felt a little sad when the wind made eerie sounds in the cracks of the doors, but I learned to think of them as the music of the elfin fiddler who sat upon the toadstool in one of the paper panels that made up the kaleidoscope of colour on the walls of my bed. On still nights I sometimes heard the rustling of a mouse in the straw under my mattress. They came and went in the cold weather and left me unperturbed because they were small and furry and utterly harmless. On evenings when there was moonlight and visitors came I was able to secure a foreshortened view of the scene through my strategic knot-hole. I could see the faces limned in the firelight supplemented by the mellow glow of the oil lamp hanging from the ceiling. I could hear snatches of conversation and bursts of laughter and sometimes the music of fiddle and melodeon when a spontaneous 'ceilidh' occurred, as it often did. Usually I fell asleep long before the evening's socialising ended, with my cat curled up beside me, as oblivious as I was to the rodine rustlings of the bedstraw mouse.

Occasionally I was allowed to accompany Grandfather, or Great Uncle Tom, and sometimes Uncle Eddie, before he was called to the colours and sent to 'The War', on beachcombing expeditions. We called it simply 'Lukkin for drift', and the propitious time was on the ebb tide after a westerly gale. It was a fascinating occupation, yielding innumerable treasures for me in the way of defunct electric bulbs, glass floats encased in net, empty tins, and pocketfuls of inconsidered trifles of flotsam and jetsam discarded from passing ships. The main purpose of the exercise was, of course, the hope of finding useful timber, and more often than not such hope was realised. Anything thus found had only to be placed above high water mark to indicate that it had been claimed, and its safety was sacrosanct until it could be carted or carried home. I often dreamed of finding a model boat, but none ever came my way. The Costie boys had several, but they were carefully guarded. I could look but not handle.

Sometimes the finds were of a less peaceful nature. Mines occasionally drifted ashore, and had to be immediately reported to the 'Authorities', and once the body of a seaman was 'whummelled' under a boat to await removal. The War was an often discussed subject, and warships were a daily sight up and down the firth. One day a floating mine was sighted in the bay about a mile offshore, and a destroyer was dispatched to deal with it. For a whole afternoon we watched, fascinated while the crack of rifles echoed across the water, and plumes of spray marked the bullets as they hit the water all around the ominous black shape. Finally a lucky shot found a detonator and a huge plume of black smoke rose into the air, followed in a second or two by an ear-splitting explosion. The shock wave rattled doors and windows and was so intense that it made me cry, and yet I felt proud to have been there. I had seen the War, and that must be the end of it! Now it was all over! Little did I know that the war had yet to wreak its quota of grief upon the family.

Soon the news came that Uncle John (Jeck) had been killed in action. Aunt Betty's husband had been killed in action; Uncle Tom, a master mariner, was missing after the disappearance of his ship, and Uncle Willie had been wounded, although not badly. Grandmother wept quietly, Aunt Daisy wept, and Grandfather did his best to restrain his grief. Being young and tender hearted I wept too for the uncles whom I had never seen, and for the kind 'feyther' whom I could scarcely remember. The fiddle hung mute upon the wall and the melodeon gathered dust behind the curtains of the 'neuk' beside the fireplace. It was a sad time when enchantment was in abeyance.

Now, with the ever-lightening days, and the cattle being led out on their tethers for part of each day, enchantment was born again. After Easter I was to go to school! I could scarcely contain my excitement. A satchel of simulated leather was unearthed from the Aladdin's cave on top of the box beds which stood back to back to form a partition between the 'but end' and the 'boy's end'. 'Abune the beds' formed a kind of loft between bed tops and ceiling, a store which accepted anything and everything that might possibly be useful on some future occasion. It was forbidden territory, even if I had been able to reach its height, a point emphasised when Aunt Daisy caught me perched precariously upon a creepie balanced upon a chair.

I was so proud of my satchel that I insisted on carrying it everywhere, hardly being persuaded to discard it at bedtime. But finally the great day arrived. A new slate in a wooden frame had been bought for me. It fitted neatly into the satchel, leaving room for my milk bottle and a 'piece-pockie', and under the solicitous care of Hugh and Rita I made my entry into the academic world. My first impression was of a muffled buzz or hum like the sound of bluebottles congregating around drying fish; I was taken by the hand and escorted to a front seat by a stern-looking lady. She knew my name, and had obviously been prepared for my coming, although I was totally unprepared for her power and authority. She strode back to her desk and rapped it twice with a pointer. Immediately a sepulchral silence descended. "Arms folded," she ordered and with a concerted rustle forty little fists disappeared beneath forty armpits. There should have been forty-two, but I failed to interpret the order and was firmly shown my duty amid a tentative titter or two, quickly quelled by one of Miss Rendall's looks. "Answer your names," came the command as she proceeded to call the register. As she did so the response, "Present!" came in varying treble tones. The register was obviously recorded alphabetically, and it was not long before 'C' was reached. "Johnnie Cooper?" came the query, and by this time I had caught the drift. "Present!" I trilled as to the manner born, and was rewarded by the ghost of a smile. No new Member of Parliament called for the first time by the Speaker felt more nervous or eventually more self-satisfied than I did after uttering that single word! I had arrived as a member of the long-awaited 'schule', and I could cope with whatever else befell.

Nothing of any great moment did befall for the first few days while I and the other new beginners were allowed to integrate into classroom and playground. I experienced the usual mixed reception which varied between contempt for a new infant, complete indifference, and solicitous 'mothering' by some well-meaning 'big lasses'. But soon my academic career was launched, and I began to learn the mysteries of putting together the sounds of the alphabet already taught by Aunt Daisy. Soon I could produce learned treatises like "The cat sat on the mat" on my slate with a squeaky pencil. In the fulness of time, as knowledge blossomed, I was called upon to fill my slate with line after line of self-accusing statements like "I must not speak in class". Such statements and cautionary precepts were usually spelled out in gradually deteriorating hand-writing after my classmates had gone home. I was not by any means a little angel!

Gradually and unobtrusively the enchanted years wore on, bringing experience, enlightenment - and disappointments as I was translated through the 'standards', from 'peedie end' to 'big end'. Meanwhile I was learning more and more about life. Under the gentle tuition of Grandmother and the sterner but no less kindly instructions of Grandfather I gained a measure of proficiency in the tasks of crofting. One of the early by-products of school was an increase in the names available for my paper friends on the back of my bed. The morning roll call supplied a satisfying list. Johnnie and Betty retained their privileged place, and, like Abu Ben Adem, their names led all the rest, but the others became Jeemos and Willos, Rubies, and Maggos. Not so Alexina, a tall golden-haired goddess who wore a perpetual floral bonnet. I considered the real life Alexina to be the most beautiful girl in the whole playground, and also the most generous. Afternoon playtime coincided with the passing of one of the island's horse-drawn vans, and it usually halted outside the school gate. Whenever Alexina had a penny or a ha'penny to spend I could be sure of a snippet from a liquorice pipe with a flaming bowl of red hundreds and thousands, or, if she could afford only a bullseye I would have a suck at it until it changed colour.

It was not only in the classroom that education flourished. The playground too had its rules, its disciplines, and its pecking order. I learned that precedence in games was not necessarily to the biggest or strongest. The leader (or the victim) was chosen from a line-up of candidates as one of the bigger children passed along prodding each in turn, and intoning the chant "Deesh - dash - duckeroo bash." The one upon whom "Bash" was pronounced was 'it' for the purposes of the game. A more sophisticated form of random selection was even more random and could not be circumvented by shuffling into the coveted fourth or fifth position. "Eetle, ottle, blue bottle," ran the legend, "Eetle ottle, oot!"

Much of my boyhood has been sketchily recorded in my writings in The Orkney View magazine, and it would be wearisome to repeat my adventures. Suffice it to say that my school days were happy for the most part. I revelled in 'compositions' where I could give full rein to a fairly vivid imagination, and it was in that direction that I found favour. My stories of a pet duck who swam into my life, and was ushered tragically out of it, did much to persuade Mr Brown, one of my teachers, that I ought to be exposed to higher education. In time he persuaded Grandfather that all the 'lies' that I wrote were indicative of a vivid imagination, and so to be accounted to my advantage. But that is another story! It has to be confessed that much of my imagination was engendered from omnivorous reading. I could spend hours on a creepie in a quiet corner devouring everything that the school library could provide and Mr Brown could recommend.

During those years I developed a penchant for composing rhyming verse. (I will not call it poetry, although it was classed as such by fond admirers). I recorded family events, mostly of a scurrilous nature, together with local happenings in long screeds of execrable doggerel, which were avidly read and filed away. To this day an occasional screed is unearthed from the bottom of some mouldering shoe-box and paraded to my embarrassment. There is no escape! I am asked, even today, if I have a copy of some piece of scurrility perpetrated sixty-odd years ago and long since forgotten! It appears that my publishers have exhumed a couple of my earlier perpetrations and have requested permission to print them. Having no wish to escape the consequences of my youthful follies, I have given my consent as an act of expiation, and in the hope that they may raise a nostalgic smile.

Eddie's Owl

When blasts o' December blew cauld on the heather,
And auld folks drew near to the peat fire's blaze,
When birds crept away from the wrath o' the weather,
To hide in some dyke thro' the cauld winter days.

Then it chanced that an owl, far away from his kindred
Had waded for weeks in the pows on the hill.
Till it happened one day the poor cattiface wandered
Close to where Eddie's sheep were enjoying a fill.

Now Ned was a hunter of great reputation.
Even mice, when they saw him, soon started to run.
There were plovers and whaups that on every occasion
Did cock up their legs at the sound of his gun.

He spied the poor owl, wi' a look on each feature
That resembled a cat on the trail o' a moose.
He threw doon his cubby and sprang on the creature
And triumphantly carried it home tae the hoose.

He showed it with joy to old John his good faither
Who said, "Giddy gad, min, whit black use is that?"
Ned said he'd stuff it, but old Da said he'd raither
"Tra the neck o' the dirt for a feed tae the cat."

Nothing daunted, our Ned found a cage for his treasure,
And so the black gibby was out of a meal,
Tho' you hardly could ca' it just much of a pleasure
The owl found his lodgings that night in a creel!

When next morning came, Ned was up bright and early,
And the owl was the uppermost thing in his mind.
He rose before six, which he did very rarely,
Tho' when porridge was going he was never behind.

He found to his joy that the owl was still living
So he shifted him into the box in the shed.
To see him great crowds of the neighbours stood shoving,
And 6d I think was the sum that they paid.

Then for weeks all the hunters in Skello were busy,
And the cattiface lacked no' for good things to eat.
He grew plump and fat and his feathers grew fuzzy.
Between sparrows and mice he had many a treat.

From east and from west to his cage men came thronging
And he looked just as happy as happy could be.
But deep down in his heart he was yearning and longing
And plotting and planning once more to be free.

When Eddie came oot one cold wintry morning,
His grief was a pitiful sight to be seen.
For all that was left the cage adorning
Was a feather or two where the owl once had been.

Then it happened one day that as Eddie was going
Past Langskaill's ley field - a most desolate place -
He looked at a spot where the gowans were growing,
And there sat the owl, wi' a grin on his face!

Little dreamed he that day of the doom that was coming,
But, poor creature, he very soon knew - to his cost!
For back at full speed wi' his gun Ned came running
And the cattiface spraggled and gave up the ghost.

Soon the body was carefully wrapped in brown paper,
And sent off to Edinburgh toon tae be flayed.
Tho' Ned's father called it - "A bonnikin caper,"
Our Eddie was not in the least bit dismayed.

When holidays came in the good Easter season,
Young Betty came home, all her old friends to see.
And Eddie was brisk for a very good reason,
For to see his stuffed owl, he was all in a glee.

Now he peacefully sits never moving a feather,
All handsome and proud on the cabinet ben,
And he dreams of the days when he walked o'er the heather
Or waded all hungry and cold in the rain.

He is happier now all his troubles forgotten,
He feels neither hunger, nor pains in his pug,
For his inside is stuffed full o' sawdust and cotton,
And in Cooper's ben end he sits cosy and snug.

Notwithstanding what has already been published by the kind indulgence of The Orkney View my errant memory continues to throw up incidents, simple and amusing, which may throw further light upon the enchanting simplicity of life before the days of radio, television, videos, and ever-menacing skateboards careering around blind corners at high speed.

One of my most precious possessions was a little wheelbarrow obtained for me by Uncle Eddie from the parents of a boy who had outgrown it. Refurbished and repainted it formed the centre piece of one of my early Christmasses. I wheeled everything movable around the brigstanes in it, including a docile old cat. My head swam with pride when I was allowed to accompany Grandmother to the van, wheeling my precious barrow with the promise that I could 'hurl' a loaf home in it. On the way to the halting place of the van we had to cross the 'muckle ditch' by a narrow flagstone bridge, or 'brig'. I negotiated it quite safely on the outward journey, but returning with the precious loaf on board, my nerve failed me! Although I retained a precarious balance, I could not control the barrow. It finished hanging from the edge of the 'brig' while the loaf landed in the ditch with a resounding splash. It was never the same again, even after Grandmother had retrieved it at the risk of wet feet. The fact that, as I pointed out, I had saved the barrow, offered scant comfort and did not rebound to my credit or my immediate popularity.

It figured again in another minor drama. I had observed how Grandfather pulled a few young turnips from time to time as a titbit for the milking cows. They had been deliberately left for that purpose, but I was not to know that. Here was an opportunity for useful service! I filled my barrow, without selecting, so that an ugly gap was left in the end of the drill, and trundled them home feeling like Jack Horner after the incident with the plum. But, unlike him, I was not a 'good boy'. I received a sound scolding and the threat of a 'flattening' if ever I did such a thing again. The milking cows were the benefactors of my wrong-doing!

Not that I had any monopoly of misfortune. A croft is a threatening place for the accident prone, with its slippery brigstanes and sudden 'swaps' of wind which can carry the unwary on to the midden; there is risk also for youngsters like me who was wont to give way to uncontrollable mirth when such things befell my elders and betters. Fortunately, fleetness of foot usually compensated for my inability to 'stop galdering'. (Grandfather's words). Grandmother too had her mishaps, like the occasion immediately prior to the arrival of Uncle Willie and one of his University friends when a tin of paint fell off a high shelf and dealt her a black eye that would have done credit to a prize fighter, and which persisted throughout the entire fortnight of the visit.

I came upon her one day, when I was a little older, in the 'milk-hoose'. It was a strange scene! She was hastily unbuttoning her tight-bodiced 'goon', and, as I watched fascinated, she eased it off one shoulder, baring her arm above the elbow. I received the peremptory order, "Boy, go in tae speak tae the minister!" It says much for my unquestioning obedience that I went, preparing an appropriately respectful grin; as I went I caught a glimpse of Grandmother's bared arm being plunged deep into a tall earthenware jar of cream. There followed a short and somewhat one-sided conversation with the minister in which I assured him that I liked Sunday School, as I liked going to school, and that I was not yet sure whether I wanted to be a farmer or a sailor, and I was seven, 'guan eight'. After that, conversation languished, but Grandmother appeared, clothed and in her right mind, and bearing a floral jug of cream. I made myself scarce.

Afterwards came the tale: caught on the hop by an unexpected call from the Rev. Cameron, Grandmother had hastily removed her 'bratt', smoothed her frizzy hair, and inserted her gleaming dentures. They dwelt normally under a 'whummelled' bowl at the top of the dresser, and were worn only in honour of V.I.P.s. A cup of tea would be called for, and for the minister only the purest and thickest of cream would be appropriate. But there was none immediately available, and she must needs take the cream jug into the milk-hoose and skim some from one of the setting pans. This was quickly done - a finger drawn around the perimeter to loose the cream, a slight tilt of the pan, and a gentle blowing to start the cream flow over the edge, and in no time the jug was filled.

If only she had let well alone! Having got the cream flowing she decided to complete the skimming into the storage jar. But time was of the essence! The minister was waiting, and she blew a little harder than was her wont, forgetting the precarious fit of her dentures, which shot out and disappeared with a muffled 'plop' into the two-foot tall jar, almost full, as the very next day was 'kirning day'. Hence her partial disrobing, for the dentures must be retrieved at all costs. To her credit, when she told the story, she gave me full credit for my emergency entertainment of the minister.

Much of the enchantment of those early years was due to the stability of her temper, and the cheerful handling of every domestic crisis. She had an infinite capacity for answering my childish questions, although sometimes she was puzzled. It took her some considerable time to identify a mysterious character called Oluvus. He was obviously a most reprehensible character for whom the minister prayed every Sunday, asking for forgiveness for him. Finally the penny dropped, and the evil Oluvus was translated as 'All of us'. Rev. Cameron had a thick Highland accent. She explained kindly on another occasion that when the sick woman touched the hem of Jesus' garment because she could not get near to him because of the press, he had not been hiding, as I thought, behind a 'press' like the one that stood against the but end wall.

Grandmother always seemed to be on hand in her capacity of advocate. She could get me out of most scrapes, or, if she failed, she could always invoke an element of mercy, so that my 'flattenings' were psychological rather than physical. Nevertheless, such was her sense of justice that when I did incur her wrath, her gentle corrections were far more telling than Grandfather's blustering threats, most of which could be ignored or blunted by discreet distance.

Thus she gently dispensed her unique quota of gentle enchantment to my formative years, even when I was a big boy of thirteen, and fully as tall as she, until one morning there was a change in the routine of the 'but end'. Grandfather hastily hung the kettle from the crook instead of the porridge pot, and blew the peat into flame. There was a sinking feeling in the pit of my stomach. Grandmother was ill! Presently Grandfather made a cup of tea and took it to her. When I got up he told me with unaccustomed mildness that she had sat up in front of a dying fire and had come to bed shivering uncontrollably, and that he was going to send for the doctor. Uncle Eddie was dispatched on his bicycle, and I could see from his face that he, too, thought it was serious.

The doctor diagnosed pneumonia, and telegrams were hastily dispatched to Aunt Betty and to Aunt Mary, who arrived towards the end of the week. Grandmother became daily worse, and the doctor, ill-equipped for such emergencies, did his best. Pleurisy set in, and the last time I saw her alive she was unable to speak to me. She died in less than a week, a relatively young woman! She died in spite of my tearful and heart-felt prayers.

On the evening of the 'kisting' with all the family gathered round I looked for the last time at that tranquil face in its white wrappings. I had no more tears to shed. I knew that with her passing the enchanted years had passed.

Aunt Betty silently placed an arm around my shoulder, and I knew that she knew that I knew.

Sooth o' the Auld Kirk

To a small boy with his feet as his only means of transport, even a relatively small island can be a big place. Horizons are narrow if one lives as I did in the valley of the west side of 'Skello', which was my boyhood's name for the district of Skelwick. My horizon was bounded on the one side by a curving brae, and on the other side by the sea. If I climbed the brae, as I often did on errands to the shop, I saw only a repetition of the scene, crofts nestling cheek by jowl, and more sea. There was even a skerry not unlike the familiar Skerry o' Wastbuist that harboured a colony of grey seals on our side of the brae.

It was always a bit of an adventure to enter the shop through the double door with its shining brass sneck, and the peremptory clang of the bell which announced each entry and brought 'Jwan' from the mysterious region behind the counter. What delightful and exotic smells dwelt within - especially when the new bread from the baker had recently been delivered and its aroma mingled with the distinctive waft from the store where sack upon sack of imported chicken meals waited distribution. A sweet and tempting invitation exuded from the drip can hanging from the tap of the treacle barrel. Many a small finger was drawn through the viscous contents, and many a dark drip fell upon ganzies as the temptation became too much and Jwan's attention was diverted. The intriguing smell of leather drifted from the rows of Herd Laddie boots ranged upon the high shelf and the frills of boot laces ready to be cut from their parent sheet. Oilskins contributed their heavy cloying quota, blending with the sharper tang of paraffin oil drifting from the steel drum outside the back door.

Visually too, the shop was an adventure ground with its rows of glass sweet bottles blending their colours with balls of coloured wools waiting to be translated into Fair Isle jerseys, and contrasting with the more sober colours of dungaree jackets and trousers, coils of rope, sacks of sugar, and paper strips festooned with rows of pins, which were given as change when ha'pennies ran out.

Perhaps the greatest anticipatory thrill in a trip to the shop was the possibility of meeting some grown-up benefactor. Everyone knew me - not that I was notorious; it was the way of life in a community where there were no strangers - and several people were kind to me remembering that my mother's death had placed me in the care of my grandparents. A penny or a ha'penny slipped into my hand would produce a collection of cheap sweets screwed into a cone of newspaper, and keep me munching happily up the brae and down the other side. There was always the diversion of Davy Hume's workshop where all kinds of interesting things went on, and there was always an array of sharp tools to be 'spiered aboot' and told not to touch because they were sharp. There were odd off-cuts of wood to be begged and whittled into some semblance of a boat. Davy was a well-known character, and well loved with it. He dearly loved a yarn, and it was said of him that when he heard footsteps passing towards the shop he would bang a piece of wood on the bench to indicate that he was in residence and feeling sociable. He had an endearing habit of repeating the last word of every sentence as if to add emphasis, and this led naturally to his being mimicked by those who had a flair for mimicry - and there were quite a few such virtuosos in Skello. We called it 'mocking', but there was no mockery in practice. At an early age I was wont to 'mock' Grandfather's somewhat pedantic utterances, which by their tone, appeared to brook no contradiction. To add conviction to his statements it was his habit to begin with "Railly, min", with the result that he was known somewhat irreverently as 'Ould Raillymin'. Grandmother too was a noteworthy conversationalist with the unique ability to maintain a continuous flow of information apropos of very little, and with a complete lack of pause or distinction between one subject and the next. One of her best remembered efforts concerned a couple of totally unconnected commentaries which went something like this: "Eddie and Davie are been tae the West Craigs an' gotten a cubbyfu' o' young aaks. Eddie hed twa o' them stewed tae his tea." Slight pause: "A'm wash'n his drawers an' gotten them on the dyke tae dry." Typical of her busy haste was the occasion when, glancing at the ORCADIAN newspaper, she announced, "Diseased Rats. Good news for Kirkwall." "MY," she announced, "that will be good news - the vile things." A glance over her shoulder revealed the necessary amendment, "Decreased Rates." She joined heartily in the laugh that followed and went gaily on to some fresh subject.

Skello was full of 'characters' who blended into a nostalgic pattern which is wholly delightful in retrospect. Some were quietly unconscious of their peculiarities where others, more flamboyant, knew their own traits and made the most of them. They tended to come into sharp focus in my early days when my world was bounded by an area which can best be described as 'Sooth o' the Auld Kirk'. The 'auld' or Presbyterian church stood roughly in the centre of the island, and for several years formed the boundary of my little world. Even Rapness was largely out of bounds until with the progress of years and the influence of school friends, I made the acquaintance of a fresh selection of 'characters'. But the sharpest and best loved memories of all belong to the people whom I could see going about their business without stirring far from home.

Old Uncle Tom of Branstane, of whom I have written elsewhere, was extremely fond of children, and was capable of gaining their confidence by his cheerful charm of manner and his insistence on being kissed by anyone under the age of five. It was something of an ordeal for the fastidious in view of his long beard and the continuous aroma of strong tobacco smoke which exuded from it, but well worth the effort because of the merry chuckle which followed the tribute. He had many grandchildren, and I think he tended to number me among them as we lived only a few hundred yards apart. He was the Session Clerk, a very senior lay post in the Kirk, and also a Sunday School teacher. During the times when we had no minister in residence, it was his duty to read a sermon, which he did with great reverence and an occasional stumble over some of the bigger words. Everyone loved and respected him, and readily forgave him for his lapse on the occasion when he fell asleep during a long sermon. As Session Clerk his appointed seat was immediately below the pulpit, facing the congregation, ostensibly to see that there was no misbehaviour by the younger members, and that adult members slept unobtrusively if necessary. Sleep was not unusual, especially at times when crofters often had to attend to calving cows or lambing ewes during the night watches.

On this occasion, Uncle Tom himself had spent a sleepless night, and it showed! The minister had been demonstrating the cleansing power of repentance to the younger members by stirring up sand in a glass of water, and allowing it to settle until the water became pure and clear once more. He should have removed the glass from the edge of the pulpit before he allowed himself to emphasise his message to the elders by waving his arms. The sleeve of his robe swept the glass from its stance. During his sudden and watery awakening Uncle Tom was heard to utter a word learned from his fishing days - a word totally out of character, and out of keeping with the conduct of worship. It created quite a stir for a few moments, reactions varying from shocked horror to irreverent titters. The Reverend Donald Cameron turned not a hair, scarcely pausing in his condemnation of sin until his exhortations were delivered to the full. It was not until he had shrugged his gown from his shoulders in the vestry at the close of the service that his great shoulders continued to shake with un-Presbyterian mirth. Such is the rigid discipline of the cloth!

Not far from my home at Newbigging there stood (and stands to this day) the local carpenter's establishment. It could only be called an establishment, for it was much more than a mere shop. It was a meeting place where those who lived Sooth o' the kirk came to order wheelbarrows and carts and kirns and cuithe wands and coffins. It was the home of the three Robbies, auld Robbie, Middle Robbie, and young John Robert. Middle Robbie was the carpenter, joiner, and undertaker, and a man of irrepressible humour, which is a trait said to be shared by many undertakers. I recall an occasion when, proceeding from his house to his workshop he tripped over the voluminous turn-ups of a pair of new P.L.Johnston working breeks and measuring his length in the mud, remarked cheerfully, "This breeks 'ill be the death o' me yet!" With a customary solemn statement of the obvious he added, "If I'm no careful I'll be doon!" His humour and sense of fun was undoubtedly inherited from his father, auld Robbie, a rotund man with a florid face like a harvest moon. It should have been a cheerful face, but it was kept in serious mould in keeping with his rather sardonic sense of humour. It was difficult at times to know whether he was serious or speaking in jest. He was, among other things, an amateur butcher, ready to oblige when a sheep or a pig was called upon to fulfil its destiny. On one well-remembered occasion I was the victim of his deadpan humour.

A sheep was being slaughtered at a neighbour's house, and where any excitement was brewing within reach, I was there. In those days before the advent of plastic balloons, the bladder of an animal was much in demand to be blown up with an inserted straw, rolled, and massaged with a view to producing the largest possible balloon which was then hung in the rafters as a trophy. There, some superstitious connection which I forget ensured some kind of future prosperity. Cheekily, I asked if I could have the bladder, and the solemn answer was, "Thoo'll get the best ane." He went on to explain that it was just the right season for the production of sheep bladders, and that he had seen as many as ten in one ewe. In faith I gratefully accepted what manifestly was a bladder, and was pressed to accept another three portions of indeterminate viscera which I was assured would blow up to enormous proportions. It was only when Grandmother discovered me in a futile attempt to insert a straw into a non-existent opening that I realized I had been hoaxed.

There was nothing he liked more than to succeed in repartee, and usually came off best when anyone essayed to bandy words with him. A relative of mine who was progressively minded ventured to give Robbie a dissertation on the qualities required in Aberdeen Angus cattle if they were to succeed in the show ring. Robbie listened patiently and issued the devastating edict, "Oh, boy, I ken nothin' aboot sic things, an' I see fae whit thoo're been sayin' id thoo kens nothin' aboot hid ither." Nevertheless, for all his sometimes acid wit, he was a man of great humanity. When a young dog belonging to Middie Robbie proved to be an inveterate hen chaser, father claimed to have cured the habit by thrashing the dog within an inch of his life (sic) with a woollen stocking!

It is one of my regrets that I unwittingly offended him in his declining years. He contracted a serious attack of shingles, an ailment beyond the skills of the local doctor, and for months endured the agony of a scarcely endurable itch which, in the vernacular of Skello, he called the 'yeuk'. I enquired after his health, and received the reply, "Boy, I'm a peur auld body, düne wi' the yeuk, an' nae use tae onybody. Whit wad thoo deu wi' me?" On the spur of the moment, remembering his penchant for banter, I replied, "Thoo wad deu tae skyle a lum." I was left in no doubt what he thought of my remark, much to my regret and embarrassment.

He recovered, however, and immortalised the sheep-dipping with one of his most trenchant descriptions. One of the adjuncts to the carpenter's shop was a communal stone tank which, in the required season was filled with a pungent carbolic solution into which the local sheep were dunked in order to rid them of pests and infections, and to satisfy the requirements of the law. Crofters came from all around leading their tethered animals, and true to the communal spirit of Skello, everyone took a hand in lifting, dunking and holding the victims over a grid to salvage as much of the solution as possible. And yet not everyone! There were those who were known to habitually arrive at the last moment and to reap the benefit of the facilities without labour. A plot was hatched: the guilty ones arrived, and by careful manoeuvring a situation was contrived where a couple of tethers were entangled behind the backsliders and the attached sheep were panicked into flight. General pandemonium ensued in which the late-comers were thrown to the ground, and by careful management were dragged through the accumulated mixture of used sheep dip and raw sheep ordure. It was indeed a terrible retribution. Old Robbie's account of the story was that, "They gaed stoorin' through the sharn wi' hid guan fae their lugs like the boo wave o' a destroyer!"

Both older Robbies have long since gone to their reward, leaving young John Robert still holding the fort as a senior citizen. I am sure that, should he chance to read this account, he will join me in an indulgent smile.

I could go the rounds of the crofts that made up the toonship of Skello, and find any number of lovable idiosyncrasies, worthy men like 'Ould Mossie', so called because his blacksmith's smithy adjoined his croft of Mossbank. Although on the verge of retirement when I remember him, he was still willing to light up the forge and to sharpen a ploughshare, or forge a hook for a cattle chain while he conversed on any subject imaginable. He was a kind of male Mrs Malaprop who was never weary of extolling the virtues of 'sibestis' as a roofing material, and 'corncrete' for building.

Perhaps the star turn of the district in the matter of spectacular achievement was Jock who lived 'doonbye'. He was an amiable man when I first remember him, possessed of above average intelligence, but with a cavalier attitude towards his wardrobe and general attitude to life. He wore whatever came to hand first each morning, much to the distress of his daughters who kept house for him after the death of his wife. He had two sons in Canada, who dutifully sent him warm clothing from time to time, although at times he found Canadian designs somewhat baffling. On one occasion he arrived at the Wednesday travelling van in a top-heavy mode. An elaborate and voluminous cardigan with an enormous rolled collar had reduced him to a state of confusion after the normal simplicity of a ganzie, and he finished by getting it on upside down with the body draped round his neck. Although accepting the top heavy drapery as inevitable he ventured the opinion that American tailors didn't have much idea of comfort, because his neck was too hot and his back still cold. But, in his phlegmatic approach to life, things didn't worry him unduly. There was always a reason for life's vicissitudes. A cup which smashed to the floor when he dropped it was condemned as lacking the necessary strength for practical use. A saucer which suffered the same fate broke because it slipped, and "Afore I could get hid aised hid was on the fleur."

The motive power on his croft, apart from the wind mill, was supplied by an ageing horse and a sturdy old ox, which was teamed with the horse for the purposes of ploughing. The load was adjusted equably by varying the length of yoke, and the whole outfit presented a spectacle of rustic adequacy and contentment. A careful observer would have noticed, however, that there were various unscheduled stops in the middle of a furrow. Again, Jock was able to account for this because of the infirmity of the horse, which suffered from a malfunction of the urinary tract, necessitating several un-productive stops before a successful evacuation. It was not long before the horse, no doubt being possessed of a modicum of horse sense, realized that if he exhibited the proper preliminary attitude he would be allowed to enjoy a rest. But he overdid the ploy, and Jock realized that he was being 'conned', to use the modern phrase. On the dramatic occasion that produced the finale Jock's exasperation got the better of him, and picking up a substantial clod from the furrow, he fired it in the direction of the horse's raised tail. Like William Tell, his aim was true, and he scored a bullseye! The horse's reaction was even speedier! His tail came down like a mouse trap, trapping the clod underneath, to his extreme discomfort. Terror gripped him at this totally unexpected readjustment of his rear end, and he set off at a wild gallop, dragging the protesting ox with him, while Jock, striving to keep control of plough and team, struggled manfully behind. An eye-witness account declared that he was dragged along with his legs flying horizontally behind him, but that must necessarily be put down to the apocryphal urge of island story tellers. It is possible to believe that the straw 'sookans' with which Jock sought to protect his trousers came undone and created the impression of a comet-like tail.

As the entourage approached the forbidding boundary of the Muckle Ditch, something must give if ultimate disaster was to be avoided. The sock had come off the plough and was buried goodness knows where. The ox was wallowing drunkenly under the pull of the coupling rein. Then a benevolent fate took a hand. Coming up against the brink of a deep ditch, the horse elected to turn to the right while the ox chose the opposite direction. An algebraic equation followed. The coupling reins held so that X equalled nothing, and the spundering couple came to a sudden halt. The horse, compelled by nature to raise his tail, unwittingly released the tormenting clod, and a modicum of calm descended on the scene.

There was no more ploughing that day. Beside the temporary loss of the plough sock, the horse was not in a fit condition to continue, nor was the poor ill-used ox, so both were led home and stabled. The insensitive ox quickly recovered his composure and was soon happily tucking in to a turnip with sounds of obvious enjoyment. Not so the horse who continued to tremble and to make unproductive attempts to relieve the pressure on his bladder. Jock decided that he would need the vet in the morning if no improvement was evident, and realizing that there was little more that he could do for the present he sat down by the fire to rest from his unwonted exercise and to await the preparation of his tea. The peat glowed warmly in the open hearth, and as he later digested his meal of bere bannock and the remains of a joint of reestit pork left over from dinner, his eyelids began to droop, and soon his beard rested on his chest.

It was almost ten o'clock when he suddenly opened his eyes and re-entered his troubled world. The horse! What was happening? At the behest of his daughter he had left his mud-encrusted boots by the outer door, but as he emerged from the 'but end' he saw that the brigstanes were dry, and decided to dispense with his boots and proceed to the stable in his stocking soles. Through the gloom he could see that the ailing animal was showing signs of improvement to the extent that he was munching hay with evident relish. Encouraged, Jock advanced to lay hands upon the horse's rump to test whether there were any signs of abnormal temperature, only to be brought up sharply by the sensation of warmth in his feet. It was only then he realized that the curative properties of nature had operated, and that a recently delivered steaming flood was flowing towards the odler. His hasty retreat came too late! Nevertheless it was with a feeling of light-hearted relief that he stamped a row of wet footprints towards the kitchen door.

The trauma of the day was over! He stripped off the wet socks and wrung them out into the hot ashes, gasping slightly at the resulting cloud of ammoniated steam. The now partly dried socks were hung on the line above the fireplace in the hope that the process would be completed before he required them in the morning. He firmly rejected his daughter's offer to wash them as being totally unnecessary. Life for Jock was uncomplicated.

Hard by the Skello Schule, on the opposite side of the road, there stands to this day a dilapidated 'but and ben' which in my boyhood days was known as Tarry Ha'. A nickname really, but no-one seemed to know its original designation. This vague identity was reflected in its erstwhile tenant, a kenspeckle figure known simply as 'Titty'. Her real name was Frances Rendall, and her father had been a doctor, but somewhere along the line she had failed to keep pace with life and had become an object of derision to the thoughtless, and an object of compassion to the thoughtful. Her pittance from the Parish was supplemented by a meagre salary paid to her as janitor of the adjacent school, and to an even greater extent by the kindness of her neighbours. She enjoyed the friendship of a limited circle of benefactors, a circle which changed in a kind of rotation, regulated by her penchant for taking the huff, or, to use the native word, 'the poots'. She was a sensitive soul, easily put out by the slightest remark which might suggest that she was in any way inferior in intelligence or behaviour. No doubt such offences were sometimes deliberate, because when a friendly benefactor was 'in' daily visits were the order of the day.

My grandmother, ever a soft touch for the under dog, was high on Titty's visiting list, and, being a kindly soul, was ever careful not to hurt anyone's feelings. It was a common sight to see a shapeless figure moving slowly down the hill, bearing her 'cloot' which did duty for a hand bag, bearing some little gift such as a well thumbed copy of The People's Friend, or, perhaps a partly consumed titbit which was not to her liking. However, the main purpose of the 'cloot' was to carry away whatever bounty Grandmother gave her. On one occasion she was absent for nearly a fortnight, and Grandmother was at a complete loss to think how she could have offended, until it eventually emerged that Titty was convinced that she had been prevented from approaching the house. A young and playful calf had been tethered in the path by which she always came, and seeing this shapeless heap of clothing, came bounding up to investigate, thus terrorising the would-be visitor. There was no way that she could pass the obstruction, as the calf's tether allowed considerable scope for manoeuvre, and which ever side Titty attempted to pass, the calf happily cavorted in front of her. The fact that she could easily have saved the situation by taking a wider diversion did not occur to her. She came by one set path, and any deviation she would have regarded as trespass. So she aborted the visit and departed in high dudgeon, declaring to all and sundry that the irresponsible and anti-social behaviour of the calf had been organised. "Hid wis some dirt id Eddie wis said tae hid," she decided. But she returned in due course, and Grandmother was reinstated. Once again the shapeless collection of rags appeared, not without a certain dignity; her movements were slow and had a quality of tattered regality. Her feet were seldom seen below the voluminous collection of petticoats, so that her progress might be compared with the movement of a haggis on castors.

Her relations with the school children with whom she

necessarily came into frequent contact were usually stormy. Children are quick to sense and exploit any peculiarities, and Titty had them in good measure. Practically every child in the playground had offended at some time. Those whose names and parentage she did not know received an accusing pointing of a claw-like finger and the threat, "Wait till I see thee mither. Thoo'll get a skelpit backside." The threat was never carried out, but thus was honour satisfied! Most of the local youngsters were known to her, as were their parents, and she refrained from threats of exposure, knowing that she would probably meet with little response. Rather, she maintained a retribution gang whom she regarded as 'hit men' and instructed any member who would listen to wreak vengeance upon the offenders. Often, in jest, she would be allowed to witness her sentence being carried out, usually in the form of a mock chastisement, and so she maintained self-respect and her sense of malignant power.

As a tribute to my Grandmother I was allowed to enter her house in order to deliver some small offering on my way to school, but entry beyond the immediate area of the doorway was virtually impossible. Apart from a narrow and winding corridor twixt door and hearth the entire floor was piled high with what can only be described as everything. She was an inveterate hoarder of magazines, papers, cardboard boxes, empty bottles and jars, old clothes too good to throw away. From time to time the local sanitary inspector, with the authority of the 'parish', would descend upon the mouldering hoard and amid raucous vituperative protest would pitch out and burn enough to allow some freedom of movement within. It took only a few weeks, however, for Titty to restore the status quo, and she was happy once more. When times were good I was sometimes rewarded with an abernethy biscuit thickly spread with butter. She scorned the use of cutlery so that the lines of her gnarled thumb shone clearly in the butter; it was easily scraped off with a pocket knife or a shard of slate, after which the biscuit became more palatable.

Being a kind of intimate 'friend of the family' I was often appointed the instrument of her wrath and sometimes given a shortlist of candidates for retribution. I took little notice, knowing full well that before the sun had set I might very well be the object of her displeasure, and there would be a contract out for me. None of us is perfect! In the fullness of time, after I had grown up and left Skello, I heard that she had succumbed to old age and had passed over. I hope that, humble though she was, the trumpets sounded for her on the other side.

Nor does she walk the Elysian Fields alone. Many of her noteworthy contemporaries have also passed on, leaving their mark upon the passing times. Not the least of these was dear old Robbie, for many years the local postman - Robbie of the high-pitched voice often raised to mark an irascibility that soon passed. Every Wednesday and Saturday his passage from Pierowall to Skello with his white pony and coalscuttle hat raised hopes of news from exiled family, or the arrival of mail order parcels from J & D Williams of Manchester. Later, the mail being sorted, he mounted his laden bicycle and began the second phase of house to house deliveries - a journey marked by occasional cups of tea, brief exchanges of gossip, and not a few high-pitched arguments. Robbie was easily moved to wrath, and just as easily mollified, and for his human weaknesses he was loved as much as for his strength as he so often had to battle against the savage winds of winter.

One with whom he could always count upon for an argument was Jock who dwelt at Roadside. Jock was a giant of a man who bulged in all directions and exuded good humour from every one of his many inches. Yet, for all his ungainly build he was a superb craftsman at his supplementary trade of cobbling. So delicate and well finished was his work that, had he lived in a previous generation, he would honourably have classed as a cordwainer. Children were often the target of his uncouth humour as they passed his door to and from school. He found great pleasure in blocking their path with his arms held wide and his massive legs apart while he assailed them with a stream of completely unintelligible gibberish. Once he had his victims thoroughly bemused he would retreat into his house laughing uproariously. As one might imagine, he was a rich subject for mimicry; indeed some of his victims were capable of giving a remarkably accurate and amusing imitation of his outbursts.

Of a completely different stamp was Tom Fergus, 'Forgis o' Clifton' in the vernacular. As a young man he had sacrificed an arm to the savage power of a threshing mill, but, with great courage and determination he refused to acknowledge incapacity, and taught himself to perform all the necessary farming tasks so vigorously and so well that it was said that he could out-do any of his workers or sons at the digging of drains. His substitute for the missing arm was a loop of rope attached to whatever tool he used and slung around his neck. His feats of one-armed strength were legendary, and it was ironic that it was his legs which finally incapacitated him in his last years, although even then he remained quiet and uncomplaining.

Less quiet was another Tom, known throughout the South end and beyond simply as 'Tammas'. He too was a big man, raw boned and powerful with a strong face that looked as though it had been chiselled from mahogany. His piercing eyes seemed to penetrate beyond the surface of life, which, in fact, his keen mind did. His opinions were forcefully expressed, and his powers of vivid description unparalleled. His commentary upon an accident where a young man had fallen from a high roof and escaped with only superficial cuts was stark and uncompromising. "Hid's a wonder he wasno' laid i' hen's meat," said Tammas. No less forthright was his commentary on a lecture delivered in the local school on the subject of poultry keeping by a Mr Corner. At the conclusion of a dissertation on the relative merits of albuminoids, carbohydrates, and proteins, Tammas was heard to declare in a voice that carried to every corner of the schoolroom, "Hid's me consuthered opinion that Mester Corner doesno' ken the hied o' a hen fae the erse o' a hen."

As a tailpiece I must relate his reaction on the occasion of the first visit to Westray of my wife. He eyed her up and down with an intentness which held not the least hint of rudeness; then after a second lengthy stare of judicious appraisal he delivered the opinion, "Jeck, like the rest o' us thoo're mibbe been a füle in thee day, bit I see thoo're haen the sense tae tak a weel-like wife." Not even her blushes disconcerted Tammas in the least!

Rest his soul, together with all the dear souls who inhabited Westray Sooth o' the Auld Kirk.

The Black and White Queyo

I canno mind noo whaur shö cam fae; hid wis somepiece i the Nort end bekase me granfaither tuk me wi him tae ca her bekase shö cam fae a big hoose an wasno wont wi a tether or bein led. Hid wis the first time I war iver been farder than the auld kirk. The village wis grand; I could hardly see hid for hooses! An shops! An folk stooran aboot wi geegs an pownies, an bicycles, an some on feet tö. Me granfaither kent immense o them an wan wife said, "An thoo're Sando's boy, are thoo?" I said, "Yas," an shö gied me a thripenny bit an I bowt a banana i Hewison's shop. Hid was tippence, and I got a hanfu o treacly sweeties wi the tither penny. I war niver seen a banana afore bit I war hard aboot them id they war fareful good, bit I thowt nothin o hid. Hid wis teuch an kind o bitter; anither boy we met telt me tae tak the ootside aff o hid. Hid wis grand efter that, bit they warno muckle o hid left efter I war gaggled hid. The treacly sweeties was ower weel, though, bit me granfaither liked them teu an I only got fower o them i the end.

Bit I war tellin aboot the queyo. Hid was a fearful big byre whaur shö cam fae. They maun been twunty kye i hid, no like wur ane id only hed twa kye an twa stricks. We got tea afore we cam hame; they war loaf an jam an Abernethy biskit an we got a blue dök egg tae piece o us. Me granfaither never eated eggs, so I eated them both, an the wife gied me a Abernethy biskit tae pit i me pooch.

An awey we gaed for hame. The queyo wasno fain o bein led an wadno go ava, bit the man gied me a piece o a bamboo cuith wand an telt me tae gie her a slerp wi hid. So I fetched her a whinner on the hench hied an she tuk hiedway an nearly tuk me granfaither wi her. Bit hid was a start an we gied ower weel till we got to Chalmersquoy. I think shö sa a bockie there, for shö was like tae gaen ower the banks when shö tuk starnwey for the sea wa. Bit I fetched her anither cleevie we me staff an we got her under wey again.

Shö sa anither bockie i the Valley o Brough. I think hid was only a teewhuppo id rais hurried oot o a pow. Bit hid wasno so bad that time bekase shö was gettin tired o trampin. When we got tae the auld kirk me granfaither hed tae gyong ahint the dyke at the back o the kirk. He said hid was "that dirt o treacly sweeties id dödno gree wi him." I were feard shö wad run aff afore he cam back, bit shö just tuk a bite o gress an chowed hid. Onywey, we got her hame a right, an me granfaither bragged immense aboot whit a gran baste shö was; he bragged a little aboot me tö, whit a gran ca'er I wur been. I wur properly brisk aboot yin, bekase he never bragged much aboot me ava.

Efter a while - I mind no hoo long - me granfaither cam in an said shö was fa'an i the been, an hid wadno be long noo. I kent somthin was lippened bekase Tammo o Branstane was pitten for bekase he kent a lock aboot kye calfin. I was bidden tae bide in oot o the road, bit whin I heard boglin i the byre, an a great ca-tö, I kent fine whit wus doin.

Whin they cam in for a peel o het water an said hid's a bull I wanted tae gong oot an see hid, bit they wadno let me. Old Tammo cam in for a peedie gless o somethin oot o the bottle i the press; he tuk aff the ould sark fae ower his ganzie, an a horrible like pair o ould breeks he hed on the tap o his tither anes, bekase they wur a weet an sharny an they wur a fareful smell wi them. Whin neebody wus luckin I slipped oot tae hae a luk at the calf. Hid wis a weet tö, an no very bonny ava. Hid wus grand efter, though, when hid was dry.

Of coorse, the next ca'tö was id the queyo wad hae tae be milked, for the calf wad need a drink. We wad likly get some beesmilk cheese tō. I hupped me granmither wad pit some raisins i hid. Hid wus aye a cast tae milk a queyo for the first time. Me granmither said mibby shö wad be better tae try hid for he was kind o coorse an hurried, and forbye he hed hands like barn cubbies. Shö got a peel an tried kind o canny, bit the first shö kent was a slerp on the lug wi a sharny tail. Shö spak kindo bairnly an flaain an rubbed her ahint the lugs an tried again; bit the queyo wasno high aboot hid an danced aboot like a cock on a het yetlin, an me granmither couldno get near her urrie ava. Efter that me auntie tried. Shö was a schule teacher an hed grand saft hands; bit na! Hid was no better.

Me granfaither thowt by this time id whit wus needed was the hand o the maister. "Gong oot o me road, lass, an sha me the peel!" Hid wus kill or cure. They warno ony trowie wey wi him. He tuk the milkin creepie i wan hand, an the peel i the tither; he set the creepie doon on the bizzie sam as he was stickin hid through the flags an clapped his backside api hid. If he haen anither hand he wad taen the queyo i hid. He clerped the peel atween his knees and got twa o the queyo's paps i his great naves. Shö niver moaved. I think shö got siccan a gluff shö wus stunned. He lukked ower his shouther at me granmither as much as tae say id he wus maister, an tak a pull at the urrie. A peedie spoot o milk cam so he tuk anither pull. Hid a gead "wullie norie" then. Maybe he was ower gevalous wi his great naves, bit shö tuk the poots an keeked oot like a horse, fetched him a whinner wi her tail, an than shö cam ower api him an laid him curlin aff o the creepie. The creepie gaed wan wey an the peel gaed the tither, an he gaed anither an lay spragglin i the odler api the keel o his back, ahint the auld coo i the next beul. Hid was the warst piece he could gaen bekase he was right ahint the hoastin coo. Shö got sic a flix id shö hoasted than; an whin shö hoasted, especially i the summer, shö wus wont tae plaister the wa ahint her. Hid wus a soond like a vot o thanks at the kirk social, an hid wasno the wa id got plaistered. I dunno think he kent whit wey me granmither an me auntie gaed oot o the byre so queek. I wur staan on the brigsteens ootby an they gaed by me just fleein. Me auntie wus lauchin till shö was lootin doon, an me granmither was lauchin that muckle shö was near gowlin. They wur lauchin so muckle hid meed me lauch tu; I wur still geeglin whin he cam oot rubbin his breeks an his ganzie wi haf o a winlin o stray. He ca'ed me a "galderin gapis" and said hid wus me id flixed her. I dudno think muckle o that bekase I wur no even been i the byre tae see the fun.

Efter that me auntie claaed her ahint the lugs an gied her twatree lumps o oilcake, an a the time me granmither was strokin the milk fae her, and shö sune got wint wi hid.

Me granmither deud pit a handfu o raisins i the beesmilk cheese, an I can fin the taste o hid yet.

Steenbrackeen

In the early days of the present century the 'Steenbrackeen' was almost a season in itself - an ever-recurring phenomenon like Voar or Hairst, or the 'Layeen doon o' neeps'. Let Philistines who have surrendered to the chanting jargon of radio and television call it stone breaking, emasculating the lovely cadences of the old Skello language. (Even that fine old word is falling into disuse; it is now referred to as Skelwick and further debased by being given a Postcode.) But no matter! To me it will always be the Steenbrackeen, the memory of which recurs each year at the time when the neeps were laid down and were not yet ripe for the singling. It was something of a sedentary occupation, exacting little in the way of physical effort, a task conducive to meditation or conversation depending upon whether it was performed alone or in company, and it took its place among the allied activities of 'ditch scooren' and 'block shifteen'.

The planning and laying out of island roads had all been completed before my minding, although not all that many years before. The 'New Road' was part of the status quo in my young life, but it was sufficiently new for the tales of its construction to be fresh around the peat fires. And harrowing some of the tales were, recording as they did the problems of converting muddy and meandering tracks into firm and straight highways. There were stories of semi-skilled essays in rock blasting, hand in hand with tales of bog which swallowed up stones by the cartload without showing any sign of filling up. One story, which I have heard repeated in recent years, recorded the efforts of an aspiring surveyor who lined up a spur road with two sighting poles without the necessary reference to a third and pegged out his road half a mile from its intended destination. Be that as it may, the 'New Road' eventually emerged as a highly satisfactory piece of civil engineering and, with the help of home-made tracks, gave access to all but the most isolated crofts. Now it rejoices in the official classification of B9066 between the pier and the South End of Rapness, and B9067 should you wish to visit Midbea and the Far West. Other roads were constructed, completing the island network, but they have been ignored by the cartographers, and left to be discovered as they meander from the Skello shore past the Tuans and the Loch o' Swartmill, and join the main road by East Gretna, thus making a pleasant loop from 'Cooper's Road' via the 'Pharay Road' and the 'Sodom Road'. Ask me not whence the outlandish and apparently unrelated names. I have always put them down to nicknames which have persisted long after their origins have been lost, but they remain as indestructable land marks, and all part of island history.

B9066 and B9067 are linked also by a seemingly uncharted road which careers steeply eastward from the now disused Midbea School, down the 'Mill Brae' past Roadmire and Smitaldy to join the B9066 to the south of the Auld Kirk. Little now remains of the old water mill which once served the West Side. Old 'Maggo o' the Mill', the widow of the last miller, remains a shadowy figure in my memory, linked with the delivery of a 'roast' of new pork when the pig was killed.

Normally my path to school was the shortest distance between two points, taking me along ditches and up the track past old Jeemie Kent's smithy - always worth a few lingering moments if the forge was responding to the wheezy old bellows, or a recalcitrant horse was being coerced into co-operation. Jeemie had a commanding vocabulary! Usually I travelled in the company of neighbouring youngsters, and we made a noisy gang, the girls usually giving the smithy a wide berth, and pretending to be shocked when Jeemie became unusually voluble. In very wet weather this path was proscribed in the hope that we would arrive at school with reasonably dry feet, and we were encouraged to go by the 'New Road', leaving a little earlier in order to traverse two sides of a square rather than the diagonal. Even then we contrived to arrive as often as not with 'sirpan' feet.

The homeward journey was a different matter. Instead of hoping for a chance meeting with our peers who came from further afield we left school with a ready-made gang and a potent recipe for mischief. There was no question of short cuts then! The 'New Road' was infinitely more interesting, and there was no time limit upon our arrival home except for the invariable exhortation, "Dunno delay," which was usually disregarded. Over the years since its completion the road had matured in many interesting ways. The deep drainage ditches were lush with grass, and the high sides where the spoil had been thrown were nature reserves in themselves, producing in their season the well hidden nest of blackbird, skylark or song thrush. The hidden runways of voles under the long grass were each a voyage of discovery deeply satisfying the hunting instinct of small boys. Occasionally the discovery of a nest of burrowing bees would produce a flurry of excitement and usually a few stings.

A favourite project when heavy rain had turned the ditches into miniature burns was to construct a dam at either side of a culvert where the ditch water was led under the road to find its way in due course to the sea. Divots of earth, or 'Feels' as we called them, were reinforced with stones, and the ditch was blocked at each side of the 'brig'. When the restricted water had reached the level of the road surface and was at the point of overflow we cajoled or bamboozled one or two of our younger companions into stooping down to see the otter which we alleged to have trapped in the culvert. As soon as they were positioned at the point of maximum danger the dam was demolished and we revelled in the sight of the victims scrambling to safety as a torrent of muddy water bore down upon them. It was all good, if not quite clean, fun, although there were occasional repercussions from irate parents whose 'drogled' infants had arrived home to report the misdemeanours of the 'big boys' - great louts of seven or eight as we were then.

The road offered other diversions according to season. In the autumn days when the ditch 'redds' had produced a waving crop of withering grass, someone always managed to buy or purloin a box of matches, and many a crackling and pungent bonfire resulted. There were few roadside fences or fence posts in those days of tethered cattle, and consequently little harm that could result from our fires. Our pyromania was passively tolerated because of the fresh crop of grass resulting in the spring, and we gave scant thought to the plight of the bank voles whose secret runs were thus exposed to the watchful eyes of the kestrels, or 'moosiehaks' as we called them. At that time a line of telephone poles ran from the Noup Head (we were told) to Rusland in Rapness, a legacy of the wartime series of look-out posts manned throughout the islands by the local Territorial force. We were forbidden to allow our fires to touch the bases of the poles on pain of being 'flattened' (in my case - no doubt other parents used other threats.)

The clay insulators which carried the wires aloft enjoyed no such protection. One by one they succumbed to a well-aimed stone, although sufficient stump usually survived to maintain the wires in place. A favourite pastime was to stand with an ear pressed to the pole, listening to the melodious humming of the wind in the wires. Some of the more imaginative of us used to declare that a constant stream of highly secret 'telegrams' was being transmitted, and we even pretended that we could decipher the messages. Naturally, those of us thus privileged were too patriotic to divulge what we had learned.

There were even times in the early summer when the ditches were sufficiently dry to serve as hiding places during our many raids into adjacent turnip fields. There is nothing more tasty than a young 'neep' grown to the size of a tennis ball. The top, or 'shaw' was twisted off, in the absence of a pen knife, and the root, wiped upon the tail of the trousers to remove the earth, and bitten off and spat out. It was then possible to peel off the skin with a thumb nail. The sweet taste of the white flesh, rendered more piquant by the astringent sting around the tongue, is something to be remembered.

Also well remembered are the threats of the owners of the plundered 'dreels'. It was not the few 'neeps' we took that they grudged, but those we uprooted and discarded as being gastronomically below par. We were very selective. No doubt many an apple orchard owner, plagued by juvenile 'scrumpers', would sympathise.

In the depth of winter the roadside maintained its diversions, not the least being the quarry from which much of the road had been built. At one corner there was a vertical cliff which overhung a pool of unknown depth, and it was necessary for every boy worth his place in the gang to traverse the meagre toe-holds of this cliff, and no dire warning could ever discourage this feat of derring-do. Fortunately, no-one ever fell in, although I can remember occasions when loss of nerve necessitated some ignominious rescues.

While I know little about the making of the 'New Road' I have a great many memories of its periodic maintenance and of my very minor contribution to the task. Although there were few motorised vehicles in those days, the road surfaces were subjected to brutal treatment from the steel-shod hooves of heavy horses and the unyielding pressures of iron-clad cart wheels, not to mention the constant erosion of rain and frost, and therefore required regular repairs. The surface consisted of broken stone, hence the 'steenbrackeen', bedded in clay and laid with a camber designed to shed surface water - a skilled process carried out in selected areas each year. The sections to be re-surfaced were decided by the local Road Foreman in conjunction with the County Surveyor who paid a twice yearly visit. No doubt then, as now, available finance was an important parameter governing their decisions, because a small army of 'steenbrackers' had to be appointed to produce the necessary metalling for the year's requirements, and the siting of the stone 'cairns' decided upon. Part of the logistics was to site the materials where a supply of bonding clay was readily available, and also as near as possible to the section to be surfaced. A further consideration was the availability of manpower to quarry and break the stone and to pile it in measurable cairns. 'Steenbrackers' generally combined the task with the normal working of a croft, and it was desirable to engage them from a suitable locality.

It follows, then, that the surveyor and the foreman had many decisions to make, and several days were spent touring the district with notebooks and measuring tape. Those surveys were apt to produce some good-natured amusement. The road foreman in our district was a gentleman of august and dignified appearance, and a pillar of his church. His stately Sunday progress in his high pony trap proclaimed him to be a model of all the proprieties, in very marked contrast to his progress during a surveying trip. That was accomplished at high speed on the pillion of the surveyor's 500cc Norton motor cycle, during which journeys the foreman presented a somewhat rakish image with cap turned back to front, coat tails flying, and his normally well-groomed beard presenting the appearance, as one local wag said, of the backside of a hen backing against a gale. But, eventually all was settled, and the foreman's dignity restored, and he faced the task of apportioning a quota of 'steenbrackeen' to each of his contributors.

My uncle Eddie was required to produce some forty yards, if my memory serves me, and child-like I was an eager if ineffectual helper. However, after a little practice, and a few blisters, I was eventually able to make a small contribution. The tools of the trade were simple and basic, consisting of a pick axe and crowbar to dislodge the slabs of stone from the 'hill quarry', a sledge hammer, or 'maul' to reduce them to manageable size, while final breaking required a three-pound hammer chisel-shaped at one end for splitting, a small rounded end rectangular hammer, and a wooden-handled hook, or 'cloorie', to draw the unbroken stone within reach of the sitting breaker. A straw-filled sack completed the stock-in-trade.

The initial operation was somewhat uncomfortable, and the first breakings tended to be driven into the ground, but it was not long before a matrix of broken stone formed a working foundation, and after an hour or so, there was a little heap upon which the padded sack could be placed, and 'steenbrackeen' proper could proceed. It did not take long to be able to spot the seams in the stone and to direct the hammer to the greatest advantage; what took a little longer was the ability to spot the occasional seam of hard 'whin' stone which was likely to yield little except blisters and probably an eye-watering flying chip. The work was not unpleasant, although it tended to be a little chilly when the north-east wind blew. Sometimes we placed the farm cart to windward in the 'cupped' attitude to provide a modicum of shelter.

In addition to the quota of normal metal there was a lesser quantity of 'patch' metal required. This had to be broken much smaller, and consequently commanded a higher price, and was used to fill potholes where a larger area of surfacing was deemed unnecessary, and was the subject of careful scrutiny on the part of both foreman and surveyor. I recall one disgruntled 'steenbracker' in Rapness who, after breaking and carefully 'shovelling up' some fifteen yards of patch, had the whole cairn rejected by the surveyor because it was too coarse. He patiently re-broke it all, although no doubt his baser instincts would have prompted him to throw the cairn stone by stone at the dissatisfied surveyor.

As Uncle Eddie (with some small help from me) had accumulated a cart load, it was shovelled up and transported to a site at the top of Cooper's Road where it eventually became a trim grey cairn worth some fifteen pounds, representing some weeks of spare-time work. Over the course of the summer, many such cairns adorned strategic spots along the length of road, awaiting the time when they were spread upon the worn surface. From time to time a supply of metal was required at a site where no 'steenbrackers' were readily available, and a different routine became operative. The road foreman had a kind of regular gang upon whom he could call, and when that happened the gang was mobilised, loaded upon horse cart, or bicycle, or sometimes two carts, together with the tools of the trade, and transported en bloc to some strategic site where for perhaps a week they would quarry from the foreshore and sit down upon their respective straw sacks and proceed to fill the air with the rattle of hammers like a massive and protracted hail storm.

I can recall some happy and carefree days at one such site at the Ayre of Swartmill, situated delightfully between loch and sea. The scene of operations alternated between a sandy shore with rock outcrops from whence came the stone, and the loch which in the summer wore a glowing girdle of marigolds, and whose margins were filled with the music of lapwings and the sharp 'pleep-pleep' of redshanks. Often a pair or two of swans added their graceful dignity to the scene. It was a happy time for me, with a new foreshore to explore between times of stone breaking. I was free to come and go as fancy dictated as my small effort was discounted in the communal whole, but I liked to join the breakers to listen to the desultory conversation and to pick up an occasional story. Equally enjoyable was the lunch time break when milk bottles and 'piece-pockies' were produced and conversation flowed uninhibited by the sound of hammers. Good humour prevailed, spiced by the occasional practical joke. One 'steenbracker' I can remember ate his oatcakes and abernethy biscuit in a gentle flurry of secret excitement because of a mysterious 'titbit' carefully wrapped in newspaper and secreted at the bottom of his 'pockie'. Anticipating a slice of cake or other exotic sweetmeat, he attempted to unwrap it unobtrusively to avoid the ribaldry of his companions, only to become the object of hilarity when his 'treat' resolved itself into a rounded stone from the pile. A later attempt on his part to reciprocate failed dismally.

Another member of the gang, an older man, yielded mirthful entertainment on another occasion by falling asleep after his lunch. One of his gainful occupations was acting as relief kiln man at the mill adjacent to his home, a task which involved sitting far into the night feeding the fireplace, or 'hoggy' of the grain drying kiln with discarded oat husks. Such fuel was reputed to add to the flavour of the oatmeal after grinding. Having enjoyed his simple repast he leaned against the upturned cart and lost himself in pleasant contemplation of the pastoral scene. His eyes closed, and by the time they reopened with a start the sun had westered by many degrees, and his companions were preparing to return home. He was devastated, not so much because he had slept, but because he had failed to deliver his quota. In spite of protestations from the foreman (a humane man) that it was all a joke, he insisted upon staying to make up the lost hours before he came home. He was reported to have been seen trudging the four miles or so at eleven o'clock that evening. Such men are rare!

Between the 'steenbrackeen' and the road surfacing there lay the ritual of assessing and inspecting stocks of metalling stone. Once more the public was regaled by the spectacle of a powerful motor cycle trailing a plume of dust along the road and bearing the somewhat diminished dignity of the foreman on the pillion. The assessment of the content of each cairn did not require the skills of a quantity surveyor. The stone was required to be piled to a statutory height of three feet, measured by two three foot poles and a length of string. The stone adopted a natural slope of forty-five degrees during piling, so that it was necessary only to deduct a yard from the basic measurements in each direction and multiply the resulting measurements together to arrive at the cubic content. There was an element of settling of the stone, but the odd discrepancy in height was ignored for the purposes of payment.

Then came the great day when a fleet of horse-drawn carts and drivers were assembled. Some were detailed to cart stone while others were detailed to dig and transport clay. The area to be re-surfaced was marked out with poles, and the foreman and a couple of his chosen assistants stood by to direct the tipping of each load and the spreading of stone and clay to the required depth, carefully maintaining the necessary camber to allow the drainage of surface water. The work progressed thus until only a yard or so of stone was left over for final levelling, and, such was the accuracy of previous calculation, that the area covered fell almost exactly within the position of the poles.

At first sight the result looked like an impassable

mess, deeply rutted by the very carts employed on the job. But wait! Do not discount the cunning of the foreman! The next task was to obstruct the newly covered road with oaken blocks, sufficiently large to impede the passage of a cart unless the horse was carefully guided. Thus, by judicious moving of the blocks from day to day, steel hooves and iron wheels were guided into prescribed tracks, until eventually every inch of surface had been well and truly compacted and criss-crossed into level firmness. It is said that the Romans were wont to compact their roads by marching their hob-nailed legions up and down day by day, until some inventive centurion conceived the notion of a heavy roller shod with replicas of marching feet, pulled, no doubt, by the same legions, thus doubling the effectiveness of the same man-power!

The blocks were removed at dusk each day, and replaced according to instructions each morning, usually by schoolboys. It was considered a great privilege to be appointed a 'block-shifter'! The payment for this responsible task was sixpence per block per week - untold wealth for the fortunate block-shifter. The positioning of the blocks was regulated each day by the foreman or his deputy. Even in those early days, mechanisation began to creep into the irksome task! One enterprising lad conceived the idea of driving a large staple into the end of each block, and then providing himself with a length of string equipped with a hook. To hook on and drag was much easier than lifting and carrying a heavy block, and so the mechanisation spread!

Accidents were few, but there were one or two inevitable occasions when either the blocks were left after dark, or a careless horseman allowed a wheel to ride up on one with the result that he was thrown off the cart and received a nasty shock fortunately unaccompanied by bodily harm, and certainly bereft of sympathy. A cyclist was, however, quite badly bruised after hitting one at speed, an occurrence which no doubt emphasised the need for vigilance.

When the compacting of each newly surfaced section was completed, the next operation was the 'scooreen o' the ditches', that is the cutting away of the accumulation of grass and weeds along the verges which might impede the drainage of surface water into the ditches. The ditches were also cleaned, or scoured, so that nothing should impede the complete drainage of the road. Considerable pride was taken in this operation, so that a newly 'scoored' section of ditch looked as if it had been cut with a sharp knife. It is a matter for regret that, like so many of the old crafts, the 'scooreen' of ditches is no longer financially viable, and we must now be content with the occasional divot removed to allow water to escape, and, indeed, surface drainage is no longer so important since the advent of tarmacadam, stone crushers, diesel rollers, and men in orange overalls, truck-borne upon rubber tyres to all parts of the island. Such is progress!

Gone for ever is the one-time thrill of dashing the half mile from our house to the 'New Road' upon hearing the sound of one of the few motor cycles on the island in order to witness the breath-taking speed of its progress, and to taste the plume of dust which rose from the dry road surface and hung in the air long after the sound of the motor had been dissipated by distance.

Yet all is not lost. If the ditches now remain un-scoured we receive our small change in the form of a greater variety of wild flowers. I am no botanist, but I find a deep pleasure in the daisies, the dandelions, the trefoils and vetches which blend with the green of the grass, together with the patches of wild mint, 'sooros' and the ubiquitous ribwort plantain, the 'soldiers' of our far-off schooldays, which no doubt are still deployed in painless battles. I can still taste the 'werchy' little fruits of the vetch, which we called 'moose peas', and ate because they looked like peas.

I wonder how many present day juvenile 'Auks' are as familiar with the roadside vegetation as we were, being transported to and from school at high speed by the school bus, or how many of them realize what they are missing. When Dora and I visit Westray we walk along the road whenever the kindness and insistence of our hosts can be circumvented, and we can decline the loan of a car without giving offence. Then we can take it all in, see it, smell it, and savour the delightful freshness of it all, free from the encumbrance of a motor, although frequently brought back to the present by the whiff of a passing exhaust. Westray being Westray, of course, passing motors frequently pull up and insist that we accept a lift. It sometimes takes quite a long time to persuade our hospitable friends that we find pleasure in our slow progress.

It must be admitted, however, that there are a great many totally alien colours in the roadside ditches these days. Competing with Nature we see the silvery gleam of a discarded lager tin with its kestrel emblem, side by side with some garish plastic carton which has lately housed some low calorie concoction, and which will now flaunt its indestructability for many months to come, or until a downpour carries it down to the sea. Present too, if less colourful, are the discarded bottles drained of some ardent spirit and carelessly tossed aside. But, lest I seem to be unreasonably critical, I must confess that my generation might have been less abstemious had we been financially better provided for. Chance might have been a fine thing! Sic transit.....!

The Egg and I

Apart from the disturbed, topsy-turvy days of the war, birds have always been one of my absorbing interests. Even then they forced themselves upon my consciousness. I recall the loathsome bald-headed vultures of Bengal, the marauding black kites (for which we had a vulgar name) of India. Mynah birds too, like starlings in Sunday clothes, trained by the tea planters of Assam to talk, squawked obscenities from the cages in the bazaars of Shillong, prostituting their God-given attributes for the profits of the greedy traders. In the dense jungles of Burma myriads of brilliant little creatures decorated the tangled branches, but there was no time to get to know them. They were not real birds to me - merely fleeting ghosts from a far-off boyhood. Occasionally the snatch of a note would echo the sweet call of lapwings in spring, the rasp of a concealed corncrake in a hayfield, or of the haunting "Coorlee" of a whaup.

In my early youth I suppose I was an 'Oologist' in a small way. I suspect that such words are convenient euphemisms for unashamed nest robbing - not that I robbed nests; I merely appropriated a sample or two for my collection. With the enlightenment of maturer years, I would gladly invest as much energy in preservation as I invested in appropriation in youth. However, I still find consolation in the knowledge that I was not a lone sinner. Several of my contemporaries shared my interest, and I am convinced that we contributed little to the total of 'endangered species'.

It is difficult to recall when first my interest was aroused. One vivid memory is of discharging an ancient and completely impotent air gun at a 'Baakie' sitting on the 'lum' while I shouted a shrill "Bang!" A schoolmaster, seeking to foster an interest in nature, lent me a book on birds, which I studied, at first perfunctorily, and then avidly as my thirst for knowledge grew. Later, I came across the corpse of a 'baakie' - probably the same one - spreadeagled ignominiously from a fencing 'stab'. I spread out the great wings, which spanned my outstretched arms. One was broken, shattered by the shot of retribution meted out for the crime of doing to a duckling what came naturally to a predator. I stretched out the partially decayed joints and marvelled at the accuracy of my bird book in its description of primary and secondary feathers, of coverts, of barbs and barbules. It was all so much more real in life (or death, in this case).

With the aid of my book, coupled with friendly instruction from my elders, I gradually learned the appearance, habits, calls and habitats of most of our native Westray birds. Blackbirds and thrushes had adapted themselves to nesting in the grassy 'redds' of ditches in the absence of their more congenial hedge-rows. Owls forsook their southern barns for concealment in deep heather, while sparrow-hawks and kestrels found homes in ledges in inaccessible sea cliffs. Sparrows and starlings found congenial hiding places under the eaves of out-houses or in the holes of drystone dykes, while scarcer wheatears, or 'chickos' raised their broods in the piles of sandy stones gathered from the fields. Once I found a robin's nest (a rare treat) in the remains of a cast-iron pot half buried by the corn yard dyke. I eagerly appropriated two of the four eggs, one for my collection, and one to swap for some other treasure. I might as well have taken the lot, because one of the barn cats found the chicks at a tender age. I caught the old 'gibbie' red-clawed, but the stone I hurled at him in my tearful rage would have mended nothing, even if it had found its mark. I never saw the robins again.

I soon found that solitary bird-nesting, absorbing as it might be, was dull, and joined forces from time to time with Hugh, a year or so older than I, but, I felt at the time, in need of the wisdom and guidance acquired from my book. Our respective homes were within hailing distance, so there was no difficulty in arranging sorties at short notice. Our expeditions were very much dependent on the requirements of our elders, because there were many little tasks required of us, and to be missing at the wrong times was apt to bring censure. Nevertheless, I suspect that there was a measure of indulgence, because we seemed to find sufficient time for our ramblings during the nesting season, happily sharing our finds.

Apart from the 'teewhuppo'-haunted fields where nests were plentiful and vulnerable during the spring harrowing, sowing, and rolling, there were innumerable nests to be found in the acres of heather-tufted moorland. We found them, marked them with little cairns of stone, and assiduously watched them from time to time until the eggs hatched. Only eggs with freak markings or peculiar colours were taken for our collections; otherwise we were as protective and solicitous as the parent birds themselves. They had more than enough problems from the predations of gulls and grey-backed crows, and the occasional swoop of a 'moosie-hawk'.

An interesting and more competitive phase of our ornithology came with the hatching of the chicks. Leaving the nest immediately they were dry, they melted into the terrain, silent and invisible, and it was a matter of both luck and skill to find a little camouflaged mite crouching with closed eyes among heather and stones while a gently and plaintively calling mother and father swooped on broad swishing wings as close to our heads as they dared. Sometimes we found a nest whose eggs were more pointed and whose base colour was more creamy than the olive-buff of the 'teewhuppo'. There was never any doubt as to its ownership. When we approached within a hundred yards the frantic 'pleep, pleep' of the redshank began and continued until we were safely out of the way.

The song of the 'lavro' (which I am now able to hear only in imagination because of ageing eardrums) seemed to be everywhere. It was fascinating to lie in the cool grass and watch a songster spiralling heavenward, higher and ever higher, while the song, adjusted by some mystery of nature, never seemed to grow fainter. Then it would flutter down silently to alight in the clover, encouraging me to fix an eye on the spot and go in search of the grey-brown eggs. It seldom worked! Most 'lavro' nests were found quite accidentally when a sitting bird was flushed almost from under foot, a phenomenon repeated in the case of 'linto' nests. The Westray linnets nested in the 'redds' of ditches too, and it was usually when we were prospecting for blackbirds and thrushes that the sudden flurry of wings and the flash of a carmine breast would indicate another 'find'. The cries of distress while we examined and admired the tiny speckled blue eggs - often as many as six - must be among the sweetest and gentlest of all bird song.

The adjacent shore was another happy hunting ground, even outside the nesting season. The tide line often produced the corpses of sea birds with whom we had little live contact, gannets, skuas, shags, cormorants, and occasional rarities unidentifiable because of ignorance or decomposition. Once there was the fresh corpse of an 'immer goose' or great northern diver - a find indeed! It occupied a prominent place in my erratically kept diary. There were plenty of ringed plovers, or 'sandloes' to be found, but it took sharp eyes to spot their four eggs among the shingle, especially when they put on their carefully rehearsed act to convince us that they had broken a wing or sustained some other immobilising mishap. Chaldros too nested at intervals along the shore where patches of coarse shingle or a crevice in the rocks offered suitable camouflage. Their nests, when found, were also marked by little cairns or driftwood indicators, and monitored from time to time. Occasionally a westerly breeze coupled with a spring tide would bring disaster to the shore nesters. Only the rock pipits, the 'banks spurros' of my youth, nesting in the grassy banks well above the tide line were immune. Their nests were easily located simply by watching them. They were birds without guile. Their nests were also marked and kept under surveillance.

Even in the dark days of winter the 'banks' could be relied upon to provide an almost continuous parade of familiar birds, redshanks, chaldros, ringed plovers, and golden plovers with the black underparts moulted, sharing the bounty of the tide line with gulls, grey crows, carrion crows, and occasionally a grey heron from the cliffs of the Black Craig of Stromness. Keeping themselves to themselves we sometimes saw a little group of what I knew as 'the bonny plovers' but which I later learned were turnstones. Belying their beauty, the feeding ground was usually a bank of well rotted seaweed, malodorously rich in maggots.

In the earlier years of our ramblings our territory was circumscribed by the distance we could travel on foot, but even then, we covered between us quite a large and productive habitat. An area of peaty bog, known as The White Moss on account of the lush growth of cotton grass, was a prolific hunting ground in the season. Carefully avoiding the 'bottomless' bog holes we crossed and recrossed the mossy hummocks which could yield a black-headed gull's nest, a clutch of ten or a dozen teal's eggs, or, as on one red-letter day a water rail's carefully concealed rushy cup with its complement of seven buff-coloured brown blotched eggs. Such a find was strictly secret, even from our friends, because the possession of such a rare specimen was a much envied status symbol.

The air over the moss was often vibrant with the undulating drumming of snipe, known to us either as 'horse-gowk' or 'mire-snippo'. We knew that their nests were plentiful, but they were difficult to find, and were unlikely to yield to anything other than accidental flushing. Any semblance of open water could be relied upon to attract a pair of moorhens, flaunting their white under-tail feathers before strutting with their dignified gait into invisibility before our eyes, leaving their eggs to our tender mercies. But we didn't rob indiscriminately. One specimen was sufficient for us!

Between the White Moss and the sea at Sandsend lay an ephemeral lochan, the scene of one of our more memorable episodes. Sadly, the lochan is no more - drained in the interest of extended pasture, but we knew and loved it as 'Ballie's loch', because it was presided over by one Balfour Miller, and it was a short step from Balfour to Ballie in the idiom of Skello. During spells of fine weather it was little more than a puddle surrounding two raised hummocks, but it took only a couple of days of rain to restore it to several acres of water, and to raise the status of the hummocks to islands. On the day in question it had rained off and on for a week, and, the outflow having been choked up by sand from the spring tides, it was a full-blown loch, and, wonder of wonders, each of the 'islands' showed evidence of bulky nests! Large black birds with white foreheads and beaks were in evidence, defying identification. Exploration was essential! Off came boots and stockings and we tentatively began to test the depth and temperature of the water. It was cold, and it deepened rapidly as we waded out. After the first ten yards or so, allowing for the sinking of our feet in the mud, it became necessary to roll our trousers to the limit, but further shivering progress indicated the need for more drastic measures. Retracing our steps, we nerved ourselves to cast trousers and drawers. I am sure that, had it come to it, we would eventually have completed our exploration in the nude, such was our dedicated enthusiasm! However, the extreme sacrifice was not called for. Gathering our sarks around our middles we were able to reach the islands without mishap. The mysterious heaps proved to be nests, containing over a dozen buff-coloured eggs similar to chaldros', but with smaller and more numerous spots. The birds, which we later identified as coot, made off with great splashing and hovered in the half-concealing vegetation on the far bank. While we gazed in wrapt amazement at our good fortune we were brought rudely back to reality by a shout, which heralded the approach of an irate Ballie. Grabbing a couple of eggs each, we once more took a double reef in the tails of our sarks and retreated hastily. Progress was retarded by the pressure of the cold water against our thighs and the clinging of the mud on our toes, but Ballie seemed disinclined to press home the attack, so that we made it to dry land with our treasured eggs intact, even if the reef in my sark had given way, to my later discomfort. It was a narrow escape! We paused to gather up our trousers, boots and stockings, but did not tempt fate by pausing to dress until we had reached the shelter of the sand dunes. There we dressed at greater leisure after seeing our tormentor making his way homeward, no doubt satisfied that he had done a good day's work. We felt reasonably safe from future repercussions as Balfour had not been near enough to identify our faces, and a study of our goose-pimpled bare posteriors could produce only anonymity - a case where hindsight would fail to produce wisdom, as it were. Miraculously, our specimen eggs had remained intact, and we felt that it had been worthwhile.

School days produced kindred spirits - boys from the south end of the island, who had access to the magical habitat of the Rapness Craigs. Officially, visits to the crags were proscribed by anxious parents, but somehow the eggs of cliff-nesting birds appeared mysteriously from pockets and caps, and were the subject of clandestine admiration and hard bargained swaps under desks during class. No doubt what we lost in academic knowledge due to inattention we gained in the knowledge of nature, but such transactions were conducted at the risk of confiscation, which was usually only temporary, as our schoolmaster was not without sympathy for our hobby. I can clearly remember the magical day when my desk-mate John produced the most beautiful egg I had ever seen, a guillemot's egg with a bright green ground and rich brown blotches and squiggles. He assured me that it had been obtained at the risk of life and limb (which was probably the truth) and therefore would command a high barter price. Haggling went on for most of the day to the detriment of our studies, and the final cost to me was a corncrake's egg, one of three found cold and abandoned during hay cutting. Although one could hear half a dozen corncrakes calling against each other during a spring evening, such was the ventriloquil quality of their call that it was impossible to locate their nests or to obtain more than a fleeting glimpse of a tawny ghost creeping through the hay, or a surprisingly large and gangling bird flying a few yards wih trailing legs.

The relationship which existed between John and myself was a peculiar one due to the time-honoured social convention of the island. We were prevented from visiting each other's homes because my uncle was courting John's older sister, and propriety forbade any open liaison between our families until the courtship had been sanctified by marriage. This union eventually took place, and all social barriers were removed, to our mutual delight, but it must be admitted that there existed a kind of semi-secret situation which we ourselves had devised opportunely. It so happened that the farm of Clifton was one that kept a breeding sow and provided the 'peedie grices' that formed the basis of the island's home-grown pork, and that an ever provident grandmother dispatched me to 'speak for' one of the expected litter. It was decreed that I should accompany 'the boys o' Clifton' home from school, deliver the order, and, on condition that I behaved myself and came home in good time, I could 'bide and play'. I had done my bit towards ensuring that the visit took place by suggesting that it would be better that I deliver the message in person lest it be forgotten by being passed at second hand. I could never decide whether Grandmother was completely without guile, or whether she chose to ignore the fact that John's home was only two fields away from Clifton. Of course he was immediately told of the impending visit, and almost before the inevitable meal was eaten he appeared in the doorway.

After a cursory look around the farm buildings, which included an inspection of the fecund sow, an enormous mountain of pork whose bulging belly almost touching the ground made her look like a monstrous haggis mounted on castors, we literally took to the hills! The four of us made such a noisy gang that we must have alerted every bird within a mile. Our first port of call was a natural loch, enlarged and furnished with a sluice as a catchment area, which provided a secondary source of water for the mill by the Rackwick cliffs. I had heard tales of 'The Hill Dam' and its bird population, but the reality far exceeded my expectations. It would be wearisome to list the numbers or the variety of species; suffice it to say that every family of wader and gull known to me was represented in strength. The bathing, preening and feeding company ranged from great sinister black-backs to dainty mincing wagtails. Discarded feathers lay like snow around the verges. The majority of birds chose to ignore us, except for the constantly piping redshanks and the lapwings executing their crazy aerobatics and uttering their sweet mating calls from sheer exuberant joy of living. We lingered while my companions, to whom this was commonplace, courteously allowed me to feast my eyes, but soon there was an undefinable sound drifting upon the east wind, accompanied by an equally undefinable and pungent smell.

I had not realised that hardly a hundred yards from the dam, over a little rise, lay Rapness Craigs of my dreams, from whence had come the exotic specimens admired and exchanged under desks at school. Wonder succeeded wonder! As we hurried towards the ever-increasing cacophony we scarcely paused to look at the nests of common terns scattered here and there among the boggy tussocks. As we reached the cliff edge a fulmar petrel, or mallimak, sailed past on stiff wings, eyeing us with arrogant curiosity. That was the first one I had ever seen, as they were at that time in the very early and tentative stage of colonisation. I already had an egg, of course! I cannot recall the price that had been exacted, but no doubt it was a hard bargain. This glimpse was but an appetiser; as we looked over the edge I could hardly take in the scene. There were birds everywhere! Gulls and guillemots crossed and recrossed, alighted and took off, squabbled and made friends again. Puffins and razorbills (coulter-nebs) whirred down to the sea to dive after fish, and others rose on blurred wings to make apparently hazardous landings on microscopic platforms, braking with feet and tails, split seconds before they struck the cliff face. And over all was overlaid a constant chorus of screams with a background of booming surf and an overpowering miasma of guano. Here was all that John had described to me - and more! We progressed along the craig from one haunt to another until we came to a 'close' where it was possible with care to scramble almost to sea level.

While my companions, hardened 'cragsmen' appeared to skip nimbly from one precarious foothold to the next, I felt that I had been brought to this dreadful place to be humiliated and branded as a coward. The occasional glimpse of the creaming sea far below produced a feeling of vertigo, but go on I must, albeit unhappily. And then, as my companions pointed, I saw a sight which dispelled all my immediate fears. In a crevice on a rock, on a huge pile of rotting seaweed and grass sat a reptilian shag. I had never been so close to a live one before and I was fascinated by the cavernous grunts emerging from the wide open yellow gape, and intimidated by its vicious pecking at the air in all directions. I was amazed at how lustrous was the green sheen to its plumage, having previously seen only flyblown corpses on the tide line. With its vivid green eyes it had a beauty which belied the apparent squalor of its nest site. I did not dare try to push it from its nest in spite of the exhortations from John, but, as it happened, around the next elbow of the rock was an exposed nest containing three chalk-encrusted blue eggs, one of which became mine while the frustrated owner grunted at me from a few yards away.

This episode did much to dispel my vertiginous qualms, and from then on I gained confidence as a cragsman - dangerous confidence as I look back on some of the escapades which have no place in this narrative. Having established the link with the Fergus boys at Clifton, it was relatively easy to gain permission for a visit, ostensibly to the farm, but in reality to the fascination of the cliffs. On one or two occasions we called at John's home in passing and sampled his sister's excellent gingerbread. Calling as a member of a gang was apparently acceptable while calling on my own was proscribed under the quaint social taboos which have long since fallen into abeyance.

It was not long before I had acquired, either at first hand, or by exchange, a specimen of every egg obtainable in the south end of the island, even including a clutch of raven's taken in the face of fierce opposition from the Point of Weatherness, when I was a few years older. These replaced a clutch of five taken much earlier and lost in unfortunate circumstances. Less than a mile from the school lay a line of low cliffs known as the Ernie Craigs, no doubt from a sometime association with the erne, or sea eagle, long since extinct as a Westray native. It was forbidden to visit them, but we often did during what we called 'big playtime' which was really our lunch time. Normally, big playtime was spent consuming our alfresco 'piece' and bottle of milk, followed by whatever game was current. Our milk bottles stood on the school window sill during the morning class, and it was a matter of keen competition and prestige to measure the depth of cream showing at the top. We even offered samples from our bottles to prove the richness and excellence of our milk, but, during the nesting season, our 'pieces' were consumed as we made our surreptitious way via ditch and dyke to the Ernie Craigs, and our rich milk swallowed unceremoniously in the anticipation of our adventure. One of the boys who lived near had reported the presence of a 'corby's' nest in a possibly accessible spot, and we could not resist the challenge.

The 'accessible' nest proved to be situated under an overhang below which there was a sheer drop to jagged rocks below - a daunting prospect beyond my cragsmanship. My contribution was to brace myself against the rock and to hold one end of a double knotted handkerchief while another boy, more daring than I, held on to the other end while he stretched to the limit of his reach and, extracting the eggs one by one passed them to me for onward transmission to the next conspirator. I think we both shook a little from the strain when it was all over, but it was with a sense both of elation and achievement that I carefully stowed the eggs in the crown of my army cap - bestowed upon me by an uncle who gratefully had no further use for it. There was still plenty of room for my head, big though it felt with a sense of heroic daring. We made our way back to school with all the stealth at our command, reaching the door just as the bell was sounding for the resumption of classes. The headmaster was waiting for us, and we knew from his stern look of censure that we were 'in for hid'. A cartoonist would have drawn us with looks of apprehension, and doubtless with rays of guilt exuding from my over-filled khaki cap. It was an inflexible rule that boys must never enter the school without removing their headgear, and while my fellow malefactors removed theirs, I was faced with a problem. No doubt the knowledge of the headmaster's scrutiny made me more gauche than normal, but while I did my best, two of the precious eggs lay in a yellow mess, rapidly spreading across the flagstone floor of the porch. The evidence was irrefutable, and the punishment inevitable. Apart from the lingering pain of the tawse, I was subjected to a further and far worse penalty. As there were now only three trophies left, and four claimants, it was decreed that I should forfeit my claim. As my erstwhile accomplices put it, "Hid wis thee bleem". With an understandable philosophy I found myself hoping that the remainder of the booty would be confiscated, but my dog-in-the-manger hope was dashed. The headmaster was an understanding man, and ravens were considered predatory vermin capable of picking the eyes from a new-born lamb.

That was possibly among the last of my egg collecting episodes. By this time I had practically completed my ambition of possessing a sample from every breeding species in the island, and ambition fulfilled, perhaps enthusiasm tended to wane. Also, about this time I was translated to what was known as 'The Burro Schule' and the quiet conducive atmosphere of cliff and shore gave place to the ever changing delights of 'the toon'. However, one escapade remains in my memory. A contemporary who had never had any part in our combined efforts located the nest of a sparrow hawk in an almost inaccessible part of the Rapness craig, and, knowing my penchant for collecting, he approached with a conspiratorial suggestion that we should try to reach it. It was Easter Holiday time, and we carefully laid our plans. It was quite impossible to reach the nest, even with a rope, but our reconnaissance showed that there was an overhanging flat rock almost directly above the nest, and it appeared to be firmly embedded. A purloined 'cuithe wand' was fitted with a kind of Heath Robinson contraption consisting of a bent table spoon (also purloined) with a crudely wire-twisted hinged cover drawn shut by a piece of elastic, and held open by a string operated from the thick end.

As my companion was of a heavier build than I, it was decided that I should lie prone upon the overhanging rock with my upper half in thin air while he lay across my feet as ballast. It was a nerve-racking operation, as there was a slight breeze blowing along the cliff face, rendering the wand almost unmanageable, but eventually I managed to coax one of the four eggs into the spoon. In my excitement I almost forgot to release the string controlling the safety cover with heart-stopping results. But eventually the prize was safely manoeuvred to the top. I suggested that for the second attempt we should change places, but it was firmly pointed out that my weight would be insufficient to provide a safe ballast - so it was 'the mixture as before'. Fortunately the second attempt benefitted from the experience gained in the first, and we acquired an egg each, which satisfied us. When, a year later, I visited the scene to see whether the sparrow hawk had returned to her eyrie I confess to a peculiar feeling in the pit of my stomach when I saw that the overhanging rock overhung no more, but had crashed into fragments at the bottom of the cliff!

It is hard to resist the inclination to write of days among the terns at Twiness, of the dunters and the gulls of Rusk Holm, of never-to-be-forgotten sorties by boat along the crags behind Fitty Hill, of dizzy visits to Noup Head (now a nature reserve), but all that is there to see and enjoy - and smell. What is missing is the charm of seeing it all for the first time with wondering eyes and enquiring mind. I can still recapture some of the nostalgic charm when my wife and I revisit Westray and are conducted hither and yonder by kind friends. We can see, and hear, and photograph - and remember. But not all the sophisticated zoom lenses, high powered binoculars, and glossy bird books donated by an indulgent family can compensate for the innocent joy of seeing for the first time an egg which you cannot even name.

I am not quite sure when my collecting finally

finished, I suppose it just tapered off. The remains of my collection were carried off in great triumph by our middle son who for a time inherited my enthusiasm, but by that time they were a sorry lot. I suppose I can claim to have retired from my erstwhile hobby with a resounding bang, although I was not present to hear it. During a somewhat adventurous winter and spring engaged in the ancient craft of kelp burning on lonely Rusk Holm in the middle of the Westray Firth, I found several black-backed gulls' eggs with unusual colouring and markings and took them, with a view to blowing and preserving them, to my 'base camp' at Rusland in Rapness. However, about that time, certain negotiations matured which took me away to a very different walk of life, and I forgot all about them.

It was not until I revisited Rusland after many years that I heard the tale of the 'big bang' which occurred some months after my departure. The forgotten eggs, unblown, had matured into bombs and in the fullness of time had blown themselves up. I was assured that all was forgiven, but reminded that the memory of me and my baakie eggs had lingered for a long time, notwithstanding open windows and innumerable deodorant sprays. It is good to be remembered!

Crafts and Cures

A chilling phrase percolates through the modern manufacturing industry, "planned redundancy". It expounds the philosophy that manufactured goods should be designed with the minimum cost and that they should be designed to last for a prescribed minimum time, after which they become redundant and are consigned to the scrap heap. "Throw away and buy new." I admit, not without shame, that, as an engineering executive of many years experience, I have been guilty of implementing this uneconomic and wasteful philosophy from time to time, while looking backwards with admiration at the men who were old when I was young - the crofters and craftsmen who inhabited my world in the early years of the century.

When they finally discarded something there was little doubt that it had fully served its purpose and that nothing more could be expected of it. During a visit to my boyhood's home I was idly rummaging in a little 'teu-fa' which once housed a rough bench where an uncle made the frames of his lobster creels and painstakingly chipped squares of stone to weight them down. The bench is no more, but an aura of things long past lingers to stir the memory. Hanging from a nail in the wall there was the remnant of a scythe blade, rusty and foreshortened, its erstwhile cutting edge serrated with tiny gashes. I remember how Grandfather gashed the edge, using a fish 'gully' of a harder temper, and how he then used the scythe blade as a hacksaw to sever the nails in driftwood when they were too firmly embedded to be pulled. Fishboxes and similar fabrications cast up on the storm-beaches found many applications once they were dismembered and dried on top of the 'henny-hoose'.

This conversion to a 'hacksaw' was the final phase

in the life of that blade. In its pristine days it had swished through the standing oats and bere, grass and nettles, keen and shining, until years of honing and dressing the end after collisions with stones had reduced it beyond the realms of usefulness. Nor yet was it condemned; rather it was taken to the smiddy to have a pivot welded to the narrow end and to have the fixing end beaten out into a spike. The spike in its turn was heated to red heat in the peat fire and burned into a length of broken fork handle, previously bored at the joiners shop with a 'wimble'. Mounted upon a four-legged trestle it then became an instrument for cutting 'neeps' for the cattle. Eventually wear and tear, plus the availability of another 'retired' scythe blade, rendered it redundant - but not yet scrapped; hence the home-made hacksaw. The 'gully' which had been used to gash the edge was restored by patient honing on the large lump of red sandstone which crowned the end of the yard dyke. This miniature boulder was companion to a smaller one - a sea-worn slab of slate blue beach stone, flat on one side and polished like marble. Upon this useful anvil was many a bent nail straightened and prepared for re-use at some future date, while from time to time it was the matrix upon which partan toes were cracked to provide an alfresco snack, or pulverised to provide food for the hens and grit for their gizzards in one tasty and eagerly gobbled combination.

The straightening of nails and the salvaging of drift wood had long ceased to be a work of necessity. It was simply a philosophy shared by all crofters that nothing useable must ever be wasted. And there, by the grace of God, go I, much to the amusement of my family, who liken me to a magpie with a penchant for hoarding screws, pieces of wire, bolts picked up from the road, and a thousand and one unconsidered trifles which they are often glad to find in my 'rumble box'.

Some of the repairs undertaken by Grandfather and his ilk would not be contemplated in these 'throw away' times. Grandmother had several large earthenware jars for storing cream awaiting 'kirning', and an assortment of large shallow pans of the same material in which she 'set' the milk to allow the cream to rise to the surface. When the process was complete a finger was 'strooked' along the edge to break the tension and the cream was encouraged by gentle blowing to descend into the storage jar. From time to time one or other of those vessels would develop a crack, requiring repair. Grandfather was something of an expert in this field. With an awl, sharpened from time to time on the sandy stone, he patiently pierced holes in the half inch thick earthenware and laced the crack with what he called 'sheutreed'. Even this 'treed' was home-made from hemp fibre and cobbler's wax, which he called 'rosid'. (This same 'rosid', warmed and rendered pliable, he used as a plaster to alleviate the open cracks in his hands during frosty weather.)

All around our croft could be found artifacts which had been recycled and given a new lease of life. A flat-tined 'tattie fork' worn beyond its useful proportions was taken to the smiddy to have its neck bent at right angles. Then, fitted with a long handle fashioned from drift wood, it emerged as a 'ware-pick' to be used to drag 'roos' of seaweed from the cart, ready to be spread and ploughed in. Half a cask from the tide line, together with a foreshortened oar from the same source combined to form a 'runging' tub for the cleaning of hens' potatoes. The other half of the cask found its destiny in the barn, filled from time to time with crushed oats, part of the ration of the 'feeders' or beef cattle whose ultimate sale contributed so much to the crofting economy.

Some of the home-made appliances failed in their function from time to time, as might be expected; one such failure, I recall, could have had serious consequences. Continuous burning of peat, supplemented with an occasional lump of coal or a log of tarry drift wood, produced a thick lining of sticky soot in the interior of the 'lum'. When portions of this fell into a cooking utensil or upon bannocks baking on the 'yetlin' the resultant flavour was somewhat unpalatable, and the sweeping of the 'lum' became a priority. Grandfather's sweeping apparatus consisted of a length of stout rope into which bunches of heather were spliced to give the impression of a jumbo-sized bottle brush. The lower end of the rope encircled a heavy stone, and before each sweeping this end was soaked in a 'pow' to shrink and tighten the knots. Grandfather ascended on to the roof via the adjacent byre, accessible by a short ladder. In stocking soles he climbed to the 'lum-head' and ensconced upon it in a kneeling position, dropped the weighted brush down the chimney and proceeded to pull it vigorously up. This process continued until Grandmother reported that the diminishing showers of soot had ceased. A final vigorous pull coincided with the slackening of the knots. The stone, freed from constraint, rumbled down the 'lum', struck the hearth with a resounding crash, and rolled across the floor to disappear under the 'but end' bed, scaring the life out of the house cats who had taken refuge there during the disturbance of their rightful sleeping place.

At the other end of the rope was Grandfather, completely thrown off balance by the sudden disappearance of any resistance. Dropping everything, he frantically clutched at the coping stones and managed to save himself from hurtling down the slope of the roof, and there he hung feeling with his feet for the ridge of the roof, both arms clutching the 'lum' in a desperate embrace. I watched, fascinated, unable to do anything to help until his feet found a grip on the ridge and he regained both balance and dignity. By this time Grandmother, severely shaken by the spectacle of the stone careering across the floor and narrowly missing her ankles, came out to assess the scene. Seeing that Grandfather was once more master of the situation she turned her attention to me and sent me packing from the scene with unaccustomed sharpness. She knew that the sight of my grinning face, promising to explode in mirth at any moment, would not be conducive to domestic harmony.

After this dramatic incident, ingenuity once more came to the rescue. The stone was retrieved and around its middle was chipped a groove deep enough to take a strong band of wire into which was twisted a ring to hold the rope. Eventually this device was superseded by a kind of bollard, complete with eyelet, salvaged from a baulk of driftwood. A recent search of 'oothooses' failed to reveal any trace, so it must be assumed that it was eventually discarded in favour of some more advanced device.

The teeming domestic hens which seemed to inhabit every available corner, including an improvised perch in the corner of the 'milkin' byre', were a prolific source of adaptable by-products, apart from the eggs which contributed so much to crofting economy, and the otherwise unproductive cockerels who formed the nucleus of many a savoury stew or pot of broth. They were the standby on the menu during the summer season of visitors and returning exiles.

I shall always remember the first time, after the war, when I was able to introduce my English wife to the delights of Westray. Arriving off the **Earl Thorfinn** we were arranged around the waxcloth-covered table in the 'but-end' and a stewed cockerel was placed in front of my wife. She naturally prepared to divide it into suitable portions for distribution, but was diplomatically assured that she had received an exclusive portion, the assurance being underlined by the production of similar portions for me and our boys. From that time on, Orcadian hospitality took on a new meaning for her - a meaning which many subsequent visits have done nothing to modify.

The plucking of fowls provided feathers for pillows and mattresses, while the stiff wing and tail 'pens' found many uses. Their stiff tips were lashed, or 'wupped' on fish hooks as lures for cuithe fishing. They were tied into tight bundles to be used as brushes for sweeping baking boards, griddles, and 'yetlins'. At times, in expert hands, they removed falls of soot from bannocks without leaving a flavour. As each 'brush' lost its pristine crispness it was relegated to the more menial function of sweeping the hearth or unearthing spiders and other 'gabloes' from dark corners. Such a bundle was a double-ended tool; the hard ends (the quills) could be reversed and used to scrub sticky residues such as porridge from the inside of pots, and, finally, all other attributes exhausted, the 'pens' could be untied and used to make sails for our little flat-bottomed boats which we sailed upon the duck pond, or, stuck into a potato to form a kind of 'sun-burst' they became a 'cripple cra' to be loosed into the wind and chased until we collapsed. (With acknowledgements to Gregor Lamb, they became a 'hen pen dirlo'.)

Goose 'pens' were treasured for the making of very superior fishing flies, whereas the quill ends, no longer required for their one-time literary role, were very much in demand for the making of 'tattie guns'. In case you have never seen a 'tattie gun', the barrel consisted of a goose quill, cut as long as its straightness allowed. It was 'loaded' by pressing each end into a potato and, with a slight bend drawing it out with a pellet inside. The other end was treated similarly, and, using a specially whittled pin one pellet was forced through the resultant airtight tube until the internal pressure was sufficient to propel the first pellet with a sharp crack and considerable velocity, preferably against the ear of the victim. After that, one end only required loading, so that a fairly rapid fusillade could be maintained until adult authority decided that enough good hen food had been wasted. But, notwithstanding restrictions, ammunition was always available, and it was not unusual in the 'tattie gun season' to see the school playground littered with sponge-like potatoes from which no more could be extracted. It was customary for all self-respecting boys to enter the classroom with at least one gun ready loaded in his pocket just in case the teacher should leave the room temporarily. Such an absence could initiate a hail of juicy pellets and sharp cracks, followed sometimes by a series of cracks of a different nature when we were caught in the act.

Progress and inventiveness produced a rather dangerous 'howitzer' version of the relatively harmless goose pen, made from the inner hollow rod of a discarded bicycle pump. These were loaded with turnip and could develop sufficient velocity to break a window, as I found to my cost! I never did discover the hiding place of my confiscated weapon!

And so the tally of adaptations and improvisations continued. Certain domestic items beyond the scope of improvisation were obtained from the local merchants, or, more often from the 'boot-guan anes' the 'tinklers' - the MacPhees and the Nowlands, and others of that ilk who made regular rounds of the islands with their pony carts, or with back packs. A 'tinnie' or small water dipper could be obtained for half a dozen rabbit skins or a bundle of rags, while the larger version, called a 'jeck' was a stage up the barter scale. A 'stroopit jeck' with a spout, used to fill the bowls of paraffin lamps, probably cost a shilling or two in hard cash, supplemented by a small joint of 'reestit pork' or half a dozen eggs. Once obtained, these 'jecks' and 'tinnies' were assured of a long tenure of life. Pot menders could be obtained from the 'van', four on a card for sixpence, but as often as not small leaks could be stopped with a dab of bere meal 'leaven' pressed into place, or, if a more permanent repair was deemed necessary, a 'luirt' of linseed oil putty was easily obtainable from the joiner's shop.

Perhaps the more traditional and time-honoured self-help projects were of a quasi-medical nature. In the absence of a resident dentist and the infrequency of such a visit, toothache was alleviated to some extent by the application of a small pellet of black twist tobacco, held in contact with the offending tooth by the tongue. The offensive burning taste certainly took the attention away from the greater pain - for a time. A slightly more effective substitute was a dab of Sloan's Liniment, although in time this too ceased to be effective. I can remember Grandfather with a steel thimble precariously balanced on the end of his enormous finger, sawing away at the jagged edge of a newly broken tooth in an attempt to blunt its effect on his tongue.

Childhood complaints were treated, often successfully, with elementary remedies. For a sore throat, what could be more effective than the stocking one had worn all day pinned around the neck! There were two cures for earache, depending upon the severity of the attack. For a mild attack, a chopped shallot was wrapped in a 'cloot' and held against the ear was considered adequate. For a more persistent bout a 'second stage' remedy was advocated. The chopped shallot was still required, but it was necessary that it should be embedded in a matrix of hot 'sharn'. In order to obtain the main ingredient in prime condition it was necessary to embark upon a patient vigil in the byre and to execute prompt action with a cabbage leaf, or 'keel-blade' at the first sign of an imminent delivery. I have never suffered the treatment myself, but I can imagine the olfactory overtones!

Apart from the ingenious improvisations of the crofters I have often marvelled in retrospect at the craftsmanship practised in the community. Several blacksmiths plied their trade in Westray. Their tools, which must now appear very primitive, were made largely by themselves from materials at hand - purpose made to suit various aspects of their every day trade. With those simple tools they fashioned the required hardware of the times, cart irons, artistically twisted pokers, tongs, which hung side by side with various sizes of horse shoes, roughed out against the day when Joe, or Dot, or Tibbie, or Bess, or some other Clydesdale would be presented to be re-shod. Ploughs were lined up awaiting new mould boards, new coulters or socks - good Westray words for the various components of the shining tool that ripped and turned the soil behind a pair of straining horses.

"S" hooks were made for stock, always in demand for the repair of cow neck-bands, ploughing chains, and a dozen other uses. While the modern smith or engineer reaches for his oxy-acetylene torch or arc welder, our less sophisticated craftsman laid his hand to the great dusty, creaking bellows and took the fore hammer. With consummate skill and judgment the components to be united were brought to the temperature where little stars appeared to shoot out of the white-hot metal. Then a knock on the anvil to remove the scale, and with uncanny skill the hammer and the components came together. A few ringing strokes and a shower of sparks and the weld was completed. Usually a couple more heats were necessary to complete the smoothing and shaping. Thus were the coulters lengthened, and socks provided with new points, or even given a complete renewal of the cutting edge, known as a 'lay'. Under the influence of improved methods it was fashionable (and, no doubt, practical) to forge a curved edge on the plough sock, so that the erstwhile flat turned furrow acquired a kind of undercut which produced a sharp edge to the furrow and facilitated the breaking up of the soil under the harrow.

The blacksmith's shop was often a place where men foregathered for a yarn and a warm. Often they would work well into the evening, the forge casting an inviting glow through the ever open door. There young farm workers off duty would learn something of the skills which would stand them in good stead when they acquired holdings of their own.

Two brothers, Timothy and George, operated a rustic syndicate by the roadside where they exhibited the kind of consummate skill which would command a fabulous salary in these times. Timothy imported huge turned cart wheel hubs from a manufacturer in Aberdeen, with the steel liners already fitted, but, from then onward each operation was done by hand. The sockets for the ash wood spokes were marked out with mathematical precision and mortised out with mallet and chisel. Each spoke was smoothed and tenoned so accurately that, once driven into place, neither glue nor nail was needed. They appeared to 'grow' out of the hub. The rim sections, or 'fulloes' were cut to a template (home made, of course) with a great wood-framed bow saw whose blade was tensioned by twisting a cord. He once told me that he had made the saw himself with elm wood handles because elm is the coolest wood to handle. What an incredible union of craftsman and tool! The 'fulloes' were mortised in their turn to receive the other end of the spokes, and halved together to form a continuous rim of exactly predetermined diameter.

Meanwhile brother Geordie had been forging and hammer-welding the steel tyres, again to exact dimensions, and when all was ready, the great day of the 'hooping' came. A circular hearth situated by a water-filled quarry was prepared. It took a considerable amount of skill to induce its six foot diameter to glow around its complete perimeter, but somehow it was achieved, and the steel hoop was laid on to become red hot, or as near to it as possible. When temperature was judged to be adequate, attention was turned to the wheel. Due to its 'dished' construction it lay flat upon two enormous flagstones, ready to receive the smoking hoop. Two stout helpers were recruited, and four pairs of tongs grasped the hoop and laid it upon the wooden rim. Amid a flurry of smoke and tiny bursts of flame it was tapped into place and 'sighted' by eye. Meanwhile a full muster of all available buckets had been filled with water from the quarry now to be dowsed vigorously upon the smoking wheel until the heat-expanded steel shrank back to enfold the wood in an unbreakable grip, which neither rut nor rock would ever break until time crumbled the wood into dust and the steel into rust.

They were unassuming men, for all their native skill. One day Timothy showed me one of his greatest treasures, a ratchet screwdriver presented to him by an itinerant tool salesman from the 'sooth'. He was fascinated by the possibility of flicking a little knob and being able to reverse the direction of its action "Wi'oot takin' me hand aff o' hid," as he proudly said. He never used it, preferring one selected from the array of tools in the rack above his bench. When I had suitably admired it he carefully re-wrapped it in its tissue paper and returned it to the drawer underneath the bench, little realizing that it was probably worth a mere fraction compared with the sharp and well-kept planes, chisels, gauges, and spoke-shaves lining his dusty shelves.

Brother Geordie was a more extrovert character, always ready for a discussion or an argument about current affairs. He was one of the few men I have ever known who could carry on a reasoned discussion without ever faltering in the execution of the task in hand. His wants were few, and his dedication to his work beyond reproach. His charges were almost beyond belief, even in those days; threepence an hour he considered enough to sustain his humble existence as a bachelor. Whatever money he found surplus to his immediate requirements he spent on books. He was, of course, a confirmed liberal, both politically and in his private philosophy. Give him an ear and he was a man inspired! He read widely and intelligently. His grasp of everyday affairs was firm, and his opinions sound and well reasoned.

In the course of his omnivorous reading he picked up a rich vocabulary of words and phrases and was obviously at pains to ascertain exact meaning and context; no Mrs Malaprop he! I have a vision of his smoke-stained face looking up from the anvil with a twinkle in his eye and enquiring as to whether there was much 'moral turpitude' in evidence in Rapness; the question was interspersed with a ringing of hammer upon anvil as he fashioned a clamp to repair a broken lever of a mowing machine, and was obviously intended to elicit the latest gossip from that end of the island.

The joinery at Muslandale was, in common with other such establishments, a place of meeting and discussion. Robbie was to be found most days (and most evenings) busy at his bench fashioning the many requirements of a crofting community - an 'assie-backet' a wheelbarrow, a farm cart, a cradle for an expected infant, a coffin for a departed neighbour. As part of his calling he was the local undertaker. His coffins were simple sombre affairs covered in black cloth while the linings were of snowy cotton. The bottoms were fitted with channels to accept the 'bearing trees' for each departed was reverently carried by their peers, two at each side, and one (usually a near relative) at the head, while Robbie in his official capacity kept time from the head of the procession. According to the weight of the burden the change-over of bearers was regulated from five to ten minutes a stint, and there were always willing hands eager to pay their respects in this practical way.

One joiner who plied his trade in a small shed by the shore was sufficiently off the beaten track that when he was working quietly his presence was liable to go undetected. But he dearly loved a yarn, and developed his own ploy to advertise his presence. When he heard an approaching footstep bound for the adjacent shop he began to beat the end of the bench with a mallet. Thus attracted, as often as not the passer-by would look in to pass the time of day. As an alternative he kept a rough log end and a saw handy, finding that a rasp was as effective as a thump.

It must not be thought, however, that all handiwork

was of a practical or essential nature. There was also much of pure artistry to garnish the mantelpieces of the crofts. Exquisitely fashioned models of sailing ships displayed the filigree of masts and ropework with astonishing fidelity, while carefully stitched cotton sails, royals, top-gallants, mainsails, jibs and mizzens gathered a patina of dust and peat reek which recalled the brown bark of the originals.

Orkney straw-backed stools graced most homes, exhibiting progressive stages of workmanship from first attempts to sophisticated poems in symmetry and regularity of curve and binding. Ships which had mysteriously crept through incredibly small bottle necks sailed stormy seas of sculptured and painted putty with white-topped waves, while exotic artifacts from the seven seas advertised the travels of past and present seafarers.

Most spinning wheels were of island manufacture, turned with infinite skill and sweat upon treadle-driven lathes. Their well-worn moving parts spoke of innumerable fleeces that had been scoured, teased, oiled, and carded before being spun into hanks of 'wursid'. Fancy knobs and other decorations immortalised the whims and fancies of individual makers, and it was a tribute to the timelessness of island life to realize that the 'gut' driving belts had been derived from the ancestors of the cats who matched the purring of the spindle with their own contented vibrations.

Nor was the creation of beautiful things an exclusively male prerogative; girls of all ages created many things, some ephemeral, like Fair Isle jumpers, others of lasting beauty, like shell encrusted trinket boxes, embroidered draw-string purses, and exquisitely embroidered table cloths. Some of these creations found a shrine 'abune the mantelpiece' while others were contributed to the Kirk Sale of Work, that annual market place and outlet for a multitude of handicrafts. It was not unknown for a garment to be made, donated, and subsequently purchased by the maker. One well-known lady had made an item of feminine lingerie known as a 'sark' to her own measurements and requirements with the intention of purchasing it for herself, and, being a lady of plain and practical tastes, she had omitted the then fashionable embellishment of lace around the neck as being "too grand for the likes o' me". A heated argument ensued when the offering was examined by the minister's sister, and was criticised for the severity of its lines. No amount of explanation would satisfy her; the fact that it was intended for the donor's own use failed to impress Miss Paterson. There could have been a crisis in the kirk, but for the patience of the old lady. She took it home, borrowed a length of lace from her sister, and tacked it loosely in position, so that its subsequent removal presented no difficulty. One wonders if there was laughter in Paradise!

It must be admitted that the cult of 'do it yourself' did not carry a guarantee of success; there were failures too, as in all walks of life, but even these were borne with fortitude, and sometimes had the virtue of entertainment value. Uncle's boots were a case in point. During the latter years of the Great War he had been drafted into an artillery regiment, and because of his farming antecedents found himself involved in horses and their accoutrements - particularly the accoutrements. He rapidly evolved an aptitude for the care and maintenance of leather goods, an attribute dear to the heart of Great Uncle Tom of Branstane who took him under his wing after his demobilisation.

'Old Branstane' as he was known, had at some time acquired a pair of wooden lasts purporting to be replicas of his rather flat feet, and upon these he had constructed a pair of very strong and handsome boots, and he saw no reason why Uncle should not emulate the feat. Uncle's feet were at least two sizes larger than 'Old Branstane's' but this problem was overcome by superimposing a couple of wooden extensions upon the lasts to conform to his requirements. And so leather was purchased and the operation launched. Uncle spent innumerable evenings with Great Uncle Tom, and from time to time was able to report progress, although there was an air of reservation in his reports.

At last the great day arrived and the boots were offered for inspection. It was obvious that something had gone horribly wrong. Either the modifications to the lasts had been over generous, or the leather had proved un-cooperative. It is difficult to remember exact dimensions, but the consensus of local opinion estimated them at a generous size fourteen. They were well stitched and obviously made to last, but the shape had somehow got out of control. I was reminded of the boots about a year ago when I beheld a glass fibre construction of the enormous footwear in which the legendary old woman lived and brought up her large family. It formed the centre piece of a children's display in a modern shopping precinct. Not that Uncle's efforts were grotesque - just larger than life!

To his credit, he wore them occasionally, their surplus accommodation being taken up with straw, which he declared to be beautifully warm in cold weather, but it was noticeable that he wore them only on occasions when he was likely to be alone. Being a man of considerable determination, it was possible that he might eventually have worn them out, had not fate intervened. It chanced that he required an urgent repair to the threshing mill, and, forgetting the enormous boots he had hied himself to the joinery. The joiner, a man of ready wit, espied them and innocently enquired as to when Uncle was going to fit the row-locks. That was the last straw!

Nevertheless all was not lost. In due course the monstrous boots were recycled. The uppers became variously hinges for a chicken house door, wear resistant sleeves for a pair of dinghy oars, and several stopper washers for stone hot water bottles, not to mention the vital part of sling-shots for me and my friends. The soles, I regret to say, failed to find a use and gradually disintegrated through rot and rust - a sad memorial to man's inhumanity to man!

A Seat on the Corn-kist

I have never regretted my brief spell of 'Farm Service', which came at a cross-roads in my life. I had completed two years at the 'Burro Schule' and due to my lack of enthusiasm for certain subjects failing to offset my alleged brilliance in others, it was decided by my elders and betters that my un-productive attendance should be terminated. Following upon this an aunt, resident in Chicago, U.S.A., who still believed in my potential, kindly offered to take me into her home so that I could avail myself of the opportunity of evening education while earning my livelihood at some employment still to be specified. Naturally, ever thirsty for something new, I was enthusiastic, and would have been off the next day, but for the fact that the American Immigration authorities had begun to put the brake upon immigrants, and had instituted a quota policy which could involve quite a long wait for a visa. In my case it was close upon two years, and, in the meantime I was offered the opportunity of serving one of the big farmers on the island. The proviso was accepted that, should my departure come at short notice, I would be released from my contract. At that time I was following in the footsteps of many of my contemporaries, but with the difference that my anticipation of farm service was limited, and, perhaps, the more enjoyable because of that.

Initially, having 'fee-ed' at the beginning of March, I was engaged for only three months, or half a term, my further engagement for a full term to take place at the May Term, provided that my work was satisfactory. My fee was to be £16 per term, with food in the farm kitchen and a bed in the bothy. Suffice it to say that I stayed for the full period of my waiting, learning much of life and discipline, acquiring the ability to live largely on little, and amassing a wealth of memories.

Those were the days when the seasons marched hand in hand with the six-year rotation of crops, when horsepower meant the power of real horses, when the hay stack garnished the farm yard and the roar of the silage cutter had never been heard in the land. The work was sometimes hard, often boring, but healthy and satisfying to a vigorous young lad, and I pursued my temporary career with enthusiasm, although not without some regret for opportunities lost; nevertheless it was this regret that spurred me to make the most of whatever lay in the future. When some four years ahead I strode proudly to the dais to receive the diploma which declared that I had graduated from one of the most prestigious High Schools in Chicago with honours, I looked back with gratitude to the time of humility which had whetted my appetite for learning.

But that was in the future. Meanwhile the stable and the bothy were at the centre of my life. Work of whatever nature was from seven in the morning until six in the evening, six days a week, with two hours off at mid-day in order to rest the horses and give them time to satisfy their gargantuan appetites. If they were stabled wet they were rubbed down with a handful of straw. It was not that they were pampered; they were simply a valuable part of the stock-in-trade. Their only rest day in winter was on Sunday, as it was in the case of the servants. The luxury of Saturday afternoon off was in the future by some years. In my humble rank of 'orraboy' I was free on Sunday, but when I was raised to the exalted rank of horseman and given charge of the Third Pair, I was required to work on a limited scale every third Sunday as well, looking after the welfare of the horses and assisting Jeemie, the cattleman. This was known as 'Keeping Sunday'.

It would be wearisome to record a catalogue or diary of farm life, even if I could. An impression of 'big hoose' farm life can best be gleaned from a series of episodes loosely linked in my memory, but still vivid, the pleasant jumbled with the boring, the hilarious rubbing shoulders with the traumatic.

My first experience had a kind of dream-like quality. I was placed under the tutelage of Jeemie, the cattleman. I was required to assist him in the morning and the evening in the byres, which left him free during the main part of the day, a situation which suited him very well, because he loved outside work. Our task was to repair the drystone dykes surrounding the fields where the ravages of sheep, cattle, and weather had dislodged the stones. I followed Jeemie blindly because the first week or so we were enveloped in a persistent sea fog which lent a dream-like quality to our activities. The scene of operations was a circle where a stone dyke stretched in both directions to a woolly infinity and on either side the mist blended into the grey-green of winter grass. We worked happily together, for Jeemie was an interesting companion - a puckish little man with a wispy beard and pale blue eyes that twinkled merrily from beneath a cap rendered multicoloured and completely waterproof from natural causes over a long period of time. He was possessed of an incorrigible sense of humour which the somewhat austere Boss was obliged to tolerate, and the majestic foreman could do no better than endure with lofty disdain. He praised my aptitude for stone work which I had acquired in some small measure from Grandfather whose chosen trade it was.

When we happened to be working near the southern boundary of the farm he would lead me to his cottage where his wife would top us up with cocoa and bread and jam. That was the beginning of a friendship which endured throughout my term of office. Part of Jeemie's emoluments, as he did not require accommodation, was the provision of a horseman and pair to cultivate his few acres in due season, and he insisted that I be appointed to the task, and that I also be appointed to deliver his annual quota of coal from the pier. This was a kind of feudal arrangement designed to supplement his fee of £18 per term, and it pleased his unassuming mind very well.

When the persistent mist eventually gave way before the west wind our vista opened and I was able to see the whole spread of fields while Jeemie taught me the geography of the farm, naming each field and catechising me until I could repeat them all - the Whin, the Lyron, the Parlour Field, the Manse Park, and all the others. An important part of my education was the situation of the gates, or 'slaps', especially those most suitable for the negotiation of a pair of carts. It was considered uneconomical to cart 'neeps' with a single cart, so the front mare was guided through the slap while the 'following' mare was trained to take a wide sweeping turn to avoid colliding with the gate post. For me this was always an anxious manoeuvre, because old Meg, my following mare, was apt to cut her corners unless watched carefully, resulting in more than one partial demolition of a dyke-end.

Old Meg played quite a prominent part in my farm life. She was a great raw-boned mare of mixed ancestry, although Clydesdale had obviously played an important part. Her light brown coat was of the texture which no amount of brushing could polish, although she loved grooming and would nuzzle me affectionately during the process. Her thirteen years translated into human terms would have made her a very old lady indeed. And, had she been human, I have no doubt she would have worn elasticated support stockings on her hind legs and would have padded around in carpet slippers. She was afflicted by an apparently incurable itching rash around her back hooves, and, as a consequence, she violently reacted to any interference in that quarter. Her hind feet were never shod, for there was no blacksmith in Westray prepared to dice with death. From time to time some attempt was made to clip her hooves with a pair of extended clippers adapted by the farrier, but it was a case of 'He who sups with the Devil needs a long spoon'.

Attempts were made to anoint her sores with a preparation supplied by the vet. This involved placing a blob of ointment on the end of a flattened stick and applying it on a catch-as-catch-can basis while she lashed out in all directions. The Boss had hitherto taken it upon himself to perform the task until she had knocked him against the wall of the loose-box causing considerable bodily harm. After that episode he decided to let well alone in the hope that someone else would be prepared to take a chance. With the brashness of youth and a desire to make a name for myself I undertook to act as ministering angel in a situation where no self-respecting angel would have dared to tread.

There was no lack of advice, to all of which I listened in much the same spirit as the hapless Job must have heard the gloomy counselling of Bildad the Shuhite, while I formulated my own plans. I had already discovered that Meg was very partial to a handful of crushed oats, and for some days I made a point of plying her with a surreptitious offering while rubbing behind her ears, a gesture to which she reacted with every sign of affection. She was really a dear docile old animal apart from her affliction. I realized that a stick, however carefully applied, was apt to irritate delicate membrane, and improved the situation by carefully washing a harness oil brush and lashing it into place on the stick only to find that it was too soft to pick up the ointment. 'Back to the drawing board'. Standing the tin in a pot of hot water from the kitchen reduced the potion to a silky softness, and a further offering of oats together with an ear rubbing session reduced the patient to as compliant a state of mind as could be expected.

The moment of truth had arrived! Before a gleeful audience of Foreman, Second Pair, Third Pair, and a motley retinue of expectant children, I administered the final caress to her ears, and, starting well away from the tender spot, I worked the loaded brush gently downwards without triggering any violent reaction. In for a penny! With all the finesse at my command I drew the brush across the vital area, scarcely daring to breathe. An ominous trembling of the leg followed, subsiding when I removed the brush. So far, so good! I liberally re-loaded the brush and tried again, this time slightly increasing the pressure and the area of operations. Meg responded with an irritable stamp, but appeared to be otherwise unperturbed. A glance towards my incredulous audience reassured me considerably and emboldened me to make an onslaught upon the other leg; the operation was rendered more difficult because the off-side leg was against the partition and required to be approached from within the danger area. Again I was successful, but it felt a very fragile success indeed. Nevertheless the task had been accomplished, and it was not without a glow of justifiable pride that I picked up the can, and together with the brush, stepped out of the loose-box. 'Stepped' is perhaps an understatement. It was somewhat nearer to flight! As I passed Meg's hind legs, some sixth sense prompted me to leap as she uttered a whinny of pain and lashed out with both feet! I escaped the worst of it as her hoof caught the tin of ointment and dashed it against the wall, but I received a splash on my ear. I tried to make light of the narrow escape with all the nonchalance at my command, but nevertheless I was shaken, although unharmed. Or was I? After a minute or so I realised why Meg had lashed out, and why she was continuing to give a fair imitation of a sword dance. It felt as though my ear had suddenly caught alight as the delayed action of the ointment made itself felt. It stung like the proverbial adder, and it took several applications of cold water to relieve the pain, and several hours to restore normal colour to my ear. I wondered what I might do to pacify old Meg, but eventually did nothing. My courage had failed me. Needless to say, my audience extracted full value from my discomfiture although I derived little comfort from their mirth. But the credit side of the episode was most gratifying; so effective had been the liquified ointment that it was quite a long time before a further application was required. That, of course, in the light of experience, was carried out in the open air!

It was not the first time she had distinguished herself, as I learned later. One of the tasks which fell to my lot was to assist the Third Pair on the water cart. That was a huge hogshead mounted on cart wheels and fitted with shafts. The well was situated in the middle of a field, appropriately enough known as the Well Field. It was a deep and dark hole which never seemed to run dry, although sometimes the water could be reached only by balancing precariously on the edge of the stone steps which led into the darkness. It was protected from the attentions of cattle by a stone surround, flag roofed and furnished with a wooden door.

It was a morning's work for the two of us to fill the barrel, taking turns at dipping the pail and handing it up to be poured into the hopper. The fact that we inevitably got very wet was partly due to natural accident and partly to mischievous tit-for-tat connivance. Boys will be boys!

When old Meg had trundled the week's water supply to its destination outside the kitchen door, the final siting was an operation requiring care. The wheels must needs rest on a certain level spot, and the stays under the shafts had to be carefully lowered on their hinges to maintain a suitable level. Only then could Meg be un-yoked. After a few essays in water carting I began to notice that when it came to un-yoking the Third Pair always found that he had some urgent task and would disappear, leaving me to complete the task. I finally extracted the reason from one of the servant girls.

Prior to my arrival on the scene he had gone through all the parking drill without a hitch but erred in that, instead of leading Meg carefully out from between the shafts, he had given her a slap on the rump which caused her to evacuate the shafts so hastily that one of her sensitive hooves touched a stay. She kicked out as was her wont and the stay was dislodged, causing the other one to swivel. Down came the shafts with a crash. The filling hopper flew off and about forty gallons of precious water cascaded into the open kitchen door. I never discovered whether it was the fond hope of the Third Pair that I might repeat the performance and thus ameliorate his disgrace, or whether it was the feeling that if anything should go wrong with the delicate operation, absence of body would be preferable to presence of mind.

So steeped are my memories in precedence and protocol that it is still second nature for me to refer to my colleagues at that time by their position in the hierarchy of the corn-kist which was dictated by the status of their horses. They have all passed on to what might be called "The great corn-kist in the sky", but their memories are still green. The Foreman always manned the first hoe at neep singling, and it was he who set the pace. Occasionally when the conversation became controversial, he might lean on his hoe in order to make a point, causing the whole field to come to a halt. Sometimes there could be as many as ten hoes when neighbours came to repay some favour and they were always welcome as much for their conversation as for the drills they hoed. At the plough, where we all worked together in one field, woe betide the underling who allowed his horses to out-pace the Foreman's pair. I recall receiving a stern rebuke on an occasion when some involuntary sound was mistaken by my pair as a signal to start while the Foreman was still engaged in filling his pipe prior to starting the next round, which we called a 'wup'. We knew our place in those days!

Nowhere was the pecking order more strictly observed than in the ritual of threshing day. The sheaf loft having been replenished from the stack yard on the first dry day (a task occupying two carts and four men for a morning) the operation of threshing could be initiated at short notice. Normally it was a task for a wet day unless the need for straw or grain called for immediate action. On threshing mornings we were required to assist Jeemie in the byres in order to free him for his duty in the sheaf loft. Only the Foreman was exempt from such a menial task. His duty was to replenish the oil tank of the engine and to fill the blow lamp and to generally prepare the massive oil engine. He was also responsible for the selection of sacks for the reception of the oats, and for sprinkling an anti-slip coat of sand upon the well-worn steps of the grain loft. We lesser mortals were convinced that he had the best of the bargain, an opinion supported by the density of tobacco smoke in the engine house. But, then, what is seniority without its privileges?

The byres having been attended to, the ritual of 'starting-up' began, and continued in a time-honoured sequence. It would have been a bold man indeed who made a premature move to upset the dignity of the Foreman's ministrations which almost attained the quality of genuflexions. A generous libation of methylated spirit was decanted into the cup of the blow lamp, and a match applied at arm's length. As the blue flame hissed and gained volume an anticipatory silence was observed until, at the predetermined juncture the Foreman commenced a vigorous pumping, and just before the flame flickered out the valve was opened and the lamp burst into a roar of pinky-blue flame. A pricker was produced and thrust into the nipple causing the flame to be replaced by an evil-smelling hiss. Anticipating this, the Foreman was ready with a match, and the roar was restored with increased velocity. It was then inserted into an opening in the engine casing, thus beginning the heating of the hot-bulb, the predecessor of electrical ignition. This preceded the Foreman's big moment! Executing a kind of critical count-down, in due course he uttered the magic word, "Right!" We all fell upon the huge flywheel, each taking station according to rank. As orraboy, and later Third Pair, my station was wherever I could lay a hand on the rim. I think my quota was little more than a gesture of goodwill.

After a minute or two of heaving and grunting the flywheel began to turn of its own volition, and a wheezing gust of exhaust gas filled the atmosphere. Then came the rhythmic "Thud-thud-puff-puff-puff, thud-puff, thud, thud, puffuff", a kind of erratic cadence which continued throughout the threshing operation. At approximately the third "Thud-puff" came the climax of the Foreman's performance. Kneeling down with an anxious expression, indicative of the risk involved, he carefully withdrew the roaring lamp, its work completed. Not a spectacular feat in itself, until one noticed the proximity of his ear to the spinning governor balls. He never failed to convey the impression that a careless move could spell disaster, although the nonchalant air of finality with which he extinguished the blow lamp belied the obvious stress of proximity to danger.

The rest of the morning's work was a cacophony of dusty noise, each man sweating at his appointed station, the Boss at the sheaf-board feeding the growling rollers, while Jeemie and I strove to keep him supplied with sheaves from which the binder strings had been cut and removed. The Foreman presided over the golden cascade emerging from the bowels of the mill, replacing full sacks with empty ones, and carrying the laden ones up the sanded steps. The Second and Third Pairs were responsible for clearing and packing the straw belching from the tail shakers and for lifting the sacks upon the Foreman's broad shoulders. My presence in the loft was a luxury for Jeemie, who was normally expected to cope on his own. I think the most impressive moment of the whole proceeding was the moment when the engine and mill were stopped and a silence fell upon the barn, like the biblical silence that fell after the earthquake, the wind, and the fire had passed, and the still small voice of calm descended.

The sheaf loft had other and more pleasant connotations, apart from affording a shadowy hiding place when, in the summer evenings, the Second Pair and I joined with the servant girls and the children of the Boss and the Foreman in rollicking games of 'Witches' and hide-and-seek. Our limbs never seemed to tire in those days, and we enjoyed our occasional evening Saturnalia. Nothing was ever arranged: such games happened spontaneously.

The bothy was a happy place. The furnishings were spartan - a couple of box beds and a few chairs, supplemented by our individual 'kists' wherein we stowed our personal possessions, and a fireplace with a generous supply of coal. In the early days of my occupancy as orraboy I was required to share a bed with the Third Pair, while the Second Pair enjoyed the luxury of a bed to himself, but on the departure of the Second Pair to another farm and the subsequent upwardly mobile shuffle, I became the Third Pair in my own right, and felt that at last I had achieved Man's estate. Occasionally we were required to double up temporarily during the lambing season when a resident shepherd required accommodation, or when a 'Hairst Hand' was recruited.

I regretted the departure of the Second Pair which broke up our evenings of song. He possessed a rich bass voice which blended well with one of the servant girls who sang a nice soprano. The other girl sang a passable contralto, while I purported to supply a kind of reedy tenor. We had all been exposed to lessons in Tonic Solfa at school, and therefore contrived to sound quite melodious. The Third Pair, as he then was, had no musical ear, but he enjoyed our singing of Moodie and Sankey hymns while he happily polished the brasses with which he was wont to embellish his harness on state occasions such as ploughing matches. He was a dedicated horseman who dreamed of nothing more splendid than a well-matched pair of Clydesdales caparisoned in polished peaked collars and jingling with brass buckles and ornaments.

At a later date singing gave place to dancing: both tuition and music was at first supplied by servant girl Kate who 'La-laed' her way through a variety of Scottish dance tunes while demonstrating the basics of Schottische, reel, polka, and the rest. I shall always remember her for her patience and enthusiasm. She was a born teacher and no mean dancer in her own right. Her cup of joy was full when a shepherd from Rousay arrived complete with melodeon and a wide repertoire of music, enabling her to give her undivided attention to the dance without having to supply the tempo as well. Happy evenings! The newly promoted Second Pair, lacking any sense of music or rhythm, declined to join in, but derived pleasure from tormenting us. On one memorable occasion he contrived to lock the door of the loft so that we found ourselves imprisoned at the end of our lesson. Fortunately my knowledge of the steading acquired during my time when I was under Jeemie's tuition stood me in good stead. There was a little used hatch in a dark corner, giving precarious access to one of the ground floor sheds. Opening it I was able to drop down and arrange a kind of landing pad with winlins of straw. The shepherd lowered the girls down while I broke the shock of their landing, and we were free once more. Naturally my first thought had been to free the door, but that had been secured by a chain and padlock normally used to deny the use of his much prized new bicycle to unauthorised children. We had beaten the opposition! Or, had we? From a dark corner came howls of laughter and a loud hand-clap of applause for the ladies' involuntary lingerie show. Our tormentor had accurately anticipated our escape route. Looking back, I am glad that he was not disappointed. Practical jokes were food and drink to him, although I doubt if he appreciated having to ride his bicycle in order to keep a tryst with his girl friend a few days later when the mysterious disappearance of the saddle forced him to ride on a potato sack wrapped around the cross-bar!

The Foreman took no part in our leisure activities, not from a sense of superiority, but merely because his domestic arrangements were more self-contained. He was a 'bowman' - bow to rhyme with cow - who enjoyed the use of a bowman's house as part of his emoluments, and lived there with his family. He received a daily ration of milk, a periodic issue of coal and oat meal. He was allowed to cultivate a few drills of potatoes for his own use, while swedes were free as was a supply of 'tail corn' for his small flock of hens. An important item of his fee was the right to graze a 'yowe' at the farm's expense, and to pocket the proceeds of her fecundity. This privilege was also extended to me once I became established as a fully fledged horseman, but between the Foreman's wages and mine there was a great gulf fixed. While I eventually received the princely sum of £18 a term, he revelled in the enviable wealth of £24! Not that he and his family lived in splendid isolation. We cheerfully helped him to harvest his potatoes and often joined him and his wife for a cup of tea, while he looked into the bothy from time to time in the summer when the stable was little used as a meeting place.

As time went on I gradually became more proficient, and under the guiding hand of the Foreman I mastered most of the routine farm tasks. He was a first class workman and was quite unstinting in the advice and instruction that he gave willingly. It was a proud day for me when I was entrusted to drive a three-horse team from the seat of a binder. No stratocruiser pilot could have felt more self-important than I, in command of three horses and the master of a collection of levers and adjustments. Like all beginners I had my share of misfortune. Old Meg figured largely in one of my more spectacular adventures. I had not yet shed the humble mantle of orraboy when I was required to harness Meg and Kitty, the Third Pair of horses, and to assist the Second Pair in harrowing the Well Field preparatory to its seeding. According to ancient custom and practice, I must needs keep one length behind my superior. In the course of our harrowing we were required to work as closely as possible to the well which I have already described, so that as little ground was wasted as was practicable. As we approached nearer and ever nearer to the stone housing of the well it came to the point where the Second Pair's harrows scraped the lichen from the stones, which meant that I would have to circumnavigate the structure. In order to demonstrate my horsemanship I guided my team to the last possible yard towards the well and with a timely tug at the left rein attempted to execute a masterly left turn. But I had miscalculated the turning circle of a pair of horses! Old Meg was forced to step backwards, bringing her sensitive legs against the drag chain, and true to her custom she lashed out wildly. The excitable Kitty, overcome by the exuberance of the moment, reared up like a wild west mustang, adding to the confusion. I rushed to the bridles in order to calm the situation, but my sudden appearance caused Meg to step backwards and to place her tender foot in a loop of the chain. The Second Pair stopped his horses and ran to my aid, and just when it seemed that nothing short of Divine intervention could save the situation, Meg lashed out again and dislodged the hook from the end of the spale, simultaneously freeing her foot from the tormenting loop. A modicum of calm descended, and by the time the irate Boss arrived panting upon the scene it was business as usual, the spale end having been temporarily restored to its place with the help of a stone from the well. The rebuke I received was surprisingly mild. The spale was repaired that evening by the neighbouring blacksmith, and the incident was closed apart from a few remarks about a certain horseman who had been observed dancing an eightsome reel with his team.

Such incidents served as talking points when we occupied our seats upon the corn kist in the darkening of winter evenings, and underlined in my memory the vicissitudes of my life as a 'farm servant'. Not that the coveted seat upon the corn kist, once achieved, fulfilled the promise of high honour with which I had regarded it in the early days. Nevertheless, with all its shortcomings, I clung to the privilege. Six o'clock remained our finishing time even in the short winter days, and we were expected to fill our time by grooming the horses and oiling their harness. Those chores were executed in a kind of low gear with frequent pauses for a smoke and a yarn. The Boss was well aware that we claimed a modicum of unofficial 'time off' and did not begrudge it. Sometimes we had come in from turnip carting when hail and sleet had forced the horses to turn their backs upon it unbidden, which sometimes caused difficulties in getting them back on a straight course again. At one time it was not acknowledged on the big farms that there was such a thing as weather; our Boss took a more humane view.

The corn kist, although sited in the only practical position, was badly placed from the point of view of hygiene. Perhaps that was why the Boss so seldom found us perched upon it, or, perhaps it was because he was always careful to signal his approach by deliberately noisy footfalls upon the cobblestones outside. Sometimes he would join us for a gossip, always being careful not to detain us beyond the magical hour of six. Old Dot, a huge Clydesdale mare, was stalled directly in front of the kist. She was an enormous animal, built like a medieval fortress, slow, docile, and permanently and noisily flatulent.

We were used to the pungent ammoniated atmosphere of the stable which, when mingled with the aroma of straw and harness oil was tolerable and not altogether unpleasant. Even the reek of the Foreman's pipe as he incinerated black twist added an acceptable dimension, but when Old Dot with a nonchalant wave of her silky tail delivered her quota of methane the atmosphere became unendurably miasmic.

As a remedy it might have been possible to have moved her a couple of stalls along, but protocol forbade: that was her place as half of the Second Pair, and any abdication of her position would have been a negation of the status quo. So what could not be cured was endured with stoicism and ameliorated by the passing of derogatory remarks concerning the build and habits shared by Dot and her groom. (The Second Pair was a large and well-nourished lad). Nevertheless the camaraderie of the corn kist remains one of the more pleasant memories of my brief sojourn as a 'ferm servant'.

During such semi-leisurely times we often found ourselves in the role of a captive audience. The Foreman had experienced military service during the Great War, and his part in the Kaiser's downfall was encapsulated in a series of anecdotes with which he was wont to regale us. Although inclined to be repetitive, he was a raconteur of some ability, with the dramatic knack of terminating each tale with the query, "An' whit deu you think o' that, then?"

On a certain blustery evening when hail was rattling on the stable window and six o'clock was fast approaching, he had just completed a reminiscence concerning the attempted conquest of a hospital sister in a Military establishment, and had triumphantly asked the punch line question. Before we could summon the customary murmur of appreciation, fate intervened! With perfection of timing never to be surpassed, Old Dot, with a contemptuous flick of her well-groomed tail, rent the air with a staccato and malodorous raspberry! I chuckled: I guffawed: I howled: I fell with a series of gasps. Finally I recovered and started the cycle all over again. The Second Pair, infected by my uncontrollable mirth, joined in. Regrettably the Foreman misconstrued our reaction and concluded that we were laughing at him, and the feast of reason and flow of soul usually prevailing on the corn kist was in abeyance. It was several days before equilibrium was restored, but eventually I was forgiven. Forgiveness was withheld from the Second Pair for a little longer on the grounds that he was old enough to know his manners.

Such trivial incidents cling in the memory like shreds of a worn tapestry, blending with the memory of summer evenings with endless twilight, and contrasting with the seemingly interminable darkness of winter. Memories of the noisy days of sheep shearing when the air was filled with the plaintive pleas of lambs unable to recognise their shorn mothers, and the distressed response of anxious ewes searching for their progeny, contrast with quiet days at plough and harrow when the 'tee whuppos' plaintively complained because we invaded the furrows where they had laid their eggs or concealed their downy chicks. I loved the plough: there is something deeply therapeutic about the soft plod of hooves and the gentle vibrations that flow through the stilts as the coulter caresses tiny stones beneath the surface. The plough virtually guides itself and the mind is free to wander where it will.

As I remember the patient plod of straining horses, a contrast comes to mind, and I remember a summer evening when the Second Pair and I had been visiting Jeemie to sample his home brew. It was past midnight when we climbed the dyke separating Jeemie's cottage from the farm. We landed in the midst of the horses, all six of them, quietly reclining with dew glistening on their coats. The two youngest leapt up, while the older and more staid beasts ignored us after a cursory glance. It was a long walk back to the bothy, and here was transport! We mounted our chosen steeds, bare-backed and bridleless. By slapping them on the neck we contrived to indicate the desired direction while a firm application of heels to equine ribs suggested that speed was of the essence.

Our mounts responded magnificently, and soon, with the resounding thunder of hooves, we arrived at the gate nearest to the farm, where our mounts were constrained to stop while we both slid over their necks and landed on the ground with considerable force. Making our way back to the bothy on the last and more staid part of our journey we were met by the Boss who, on his way to bed, had heard the thunder of our approach. We were caught red handed (and red faced) and subjected to a lecture during which strong sentiment begat strong words. Again the Second Pair, being the older, bore the brunt of the rebuke.

We were not by any means incarcerated on the farm, and often set off on our bicycles in search of companionship and adventure: in the village shop we met our counterparts from other farms and exchanged farm and other gossip over bottles of lemonade or the more fashionable American Cream Soda. Whatever the label said, they tasted the same, and when freshly opened the bubbles of escaping carbon dioxide tickled our noses and made us 'rift' noisily. Those social gatherings culminated twice a year, on term night, in a Bacchanalian orgy when we had been paid and felt plutocratically wealthy. The morrow would serve to pay for boots and shirts and socks purchased 'on the slate' but Term Night was for celebration. Some of the older men would form a syndicate to purchase a 'flattie' of whisky and to share it in the hope that it would induce some mystical feeling of well-being. The well-being, although imaginary, served its purpose: there was not enough to go round with any effect.

We more abstemious mortals contented ourselves by syndicating a Dundee cake and dividing it with the aid of a pocket knife, and felt that we had had a whale of a time. A quarter of caramels completed the festival, and if we could find a damsel willing to sit on the wall by the shore and share them with us, so much the better. I recall one lad, the son of a widowed mother, who tried to compensate for six months of meagre food in a 'bad' situation. He purchased a two-shilling cake of the type known as Scotch Bun, and proceeded to demolish it single handed, scorning any mechanical aid, while crumbs from the pastry casing showered all and sundry. No syndicate for him! Knowing his circumstances, no-one made fun of him, and he continued his orgy to the limit of his capacity. Or, perhaps it was the limit of his conscience. We realized when he asked for a 'pockie' that the remaining portion of his feast was destined to be an offering for his mother, together with the greater portion of his half year's wages after he had deducted enough to pay his debts for the necessities of life. Next day he was due to start work at a farm with a reputation for a generous table, and we all wished him well!

Shortly after this incident the call came from the American Embassy in Glasgow, and, having had some advance warning, my replacement was already installed in the bothy, and I finished where I had begun, an orraboy once more, my seat on the corn kist vacated for ever!

The Last of the Holmie Boys

The Green Holms lay behind us in the path of the June sunlight which lit the slopes of Fersness Hill to starboard. The M.V.**Orcadia** made steady progress towards Faray with a scarcely perceptible roll while my wife and I leaned against the port rail in relaxed mood, looking forward with keen anticipation to our first retirement holiday, a pilgrimage to my native Westray. Rusk Holm lay low between us and the Ness of Rapness, its twin humps of the 'Fort' and the 'Hoose' almost in line. A lady, obviously a visitor fae 'sooth', examined the Holm through binoculars and remarked to no-one in particular that it must be inhabited because there was a building and there were children playing. I felt constrained to explain to her that the "children" were native Orkney sheep, and when she gave that "how do you know?" look I felt obliged to expand my statement.

Memories came easily on that lovely June morning and, almost thinking aloud, I found myself telling of another May and June, back in 1933 when Danny, Jim and I had wrested a year's livelihood out of the tangles and ware cast up on the rugged shores of the Holm. I saw again the sparse grass covered with a rich carpet of drying seaweed surrounding the shallow stonelined kiln where we burned it, kilns over a foot deep in the peaty soil, and round and as big as cart wheels. Marine biologists would have called it furbelows, but to us it was simply ware, a raw material to be collected after each tide, and carried up from the rocky geos on "ware barrows", stretcher-like frames with a wire cage at the centre, capable of carrying two or three hundredweights of wet weed. These we carried over slippery rocks and through "pows" until it seemed sometimes that our arms must surely part from our shoulders - but we were young, revelling in our strength. In fact we often overdid our loading because no-one would be the first to say "enough". Hour after hour we toiled until the whole of the foreshore was covered.

Then it became a time of anxious weather forecasting; a dry spell of weather was essential to the quality of our harvest. It had to be tinder dry in order to burn, and we also believed that rain washed some of the 'goodness' out of the ware. Not only must it be flammable in its own right, but it also had to be capable of aiding the combustion of the tons of tangles which we had collected during the storms of winter and piled 'hieds an tras' on stone 'steaths' to dry into gnarled and wizened thongs.

As the **Orcadia** swung to starboard to enter Faray Sound I saw again, in imagination, plumes of smoke rising from kelp kilns all around - from Eday, from Faray, from Rapness and Twiness - the pungent reek blending and fading eastwards until it was lost in the blue of Sanday's sky. I heard again the crackle, saw again the spurting flame, and remembered how each spurt must immediately be covered with a forkful of ware or an armful of tangles; good kelp had to be roasted like charcoal rather than burned.

Kelp burning was a skilled job requiring knowledge handed down from generation to generation. It is said that the first exponents of the craft in Orkney insisted that the making of good kelp involved the muttering of an incantation! However, we coped without the aid of the supernatural, and with no lack of success. Danny and I handled a kiln each while Jim, the youngest member of the team, acted as cook and part-time raw material carrier. It was hard work, and the hours were long; often it was nearly midnight before a kiln was run down, stirred into a semi-liquid jelly, and left to cool slowly. After a couple of days it was ready to 'raise'; this involved the use of a crowbar if the kiln had set well. The kelp sometimes came up in a solid cake weighing several hundredweights; then it had to be broken into manageable portions and transported on the ubiquitous hand barrow to be stored in the 'hoose', the other end of which was our living quarters.

We lived simply and ate prodigiously from the 'holmie boxes' of provisions supplied by our shore-based sponsors, and replenished during the week-end trips ashore. Sometimes Jim produced an essay into "haute cuisine" when he executed an enormous omelette with eggs supplied under raucous protests by our resident colony of 'scories'. He was an expert at selecting new-laid specimens, although there were occasional lapses in his water-testing methods.

We lived very close to nature. Common seals (actually not very common) came ashore to give birth to lovely snowy pups, all full of innocence, and weeping great sad tears as they waited for their mothers to come and suckle them. The mothers learned to tolerate our presence on a "let be for let be" basis, but there was never complete rapport, a situation also obtaining in our relationship with the flock of 'holmie' sheep which thrived by browsing 'tang' among the rocks of foreshore and skerry. It was noticeable that no ewe would ever allow us to get between her and her lamb. More trusting was "Auld Kirsie", a matronly dunter who brooded her four eggs in a downy nest beside the pool of brackish and muddy water in the centre of the Holm, known simply as 'the pow'. As we passed her nest we were allowed to stroke her head until the ducklings hatched and her hormone-induced tranquillity was overtaken by the protective instinct of motherhood. Jim was the victim; he found his friendly gesture repelled with venom and vigour. As I recall, there was bloodshed. Regrettably, only one of her offspring survived the predation of the blackbacks.

Every day we worked we were attended by clouds of common and Arctic terns. They floated in and out of the smoke like little snowflakes, and their grating cries were a constant background. Tysties also found the Holm a congenial habitat, and in the evening, when leisure allowed we could locate the nests of dozens of storm petrels by their 'churring' emerging from gaps in the sheep dykes. Gulls of several types abounded, and many flights and rafts of auks and tammie-nories from the Rapness cliffs passed by on their fishing forays.

Gradually our store of kelp accumulated; weeks on

the Holm alternated with spells of farm work, depending upon the strength and airt of the wind which regulated our supply of ware. Those spells of farm work were a welcome change from the austerity of the Holm. The varying activities of spring offered variety - harrowing, sowing, shifting fences to regulate the usage of fields for pasture or hay. There was no silage in those days; good old-fashioned 'neeps' provided a large part of indoor cattle feed. Perhaps the most satisfactory part of land-based activity was the comfort of a feather bed, and the bounty of Rusland's table. No disrespect is intended towards Jim's catering, but the difference in the quality of preparation was noticeable, and perhaps the flavour of potatoes boiled in fresh water had the edge over those boiled in water from the Westray Firth. The evenings too, were more lightsome in the company of a larger choice of companions, not to mention the spontaneous ceilidhs when John o' Rusland on the fiddle, a visitor on the accordion, and myself on the guitar indulged in an extended repertoire of Scottish dance music. Among my egg-collecting acquaintances there were many requests for exotic specimens from the isolated rocks and beaches of the Holm; I was able from time to time to execute some advantageous 'swaps'.

"How did you get into this in the first place?" my one-lady audience enquired. By this time the **Orcadia** was clearing the Faray Holm, and the point of Weatherness lay ahead on the port quarter with the south end of Rapness spread out to westward. There on its hill I was able to point out the farm of Rusland. I told how in a time of scarce employment a chance remark about the long discontinued kelp burning expeditions to Rusk Holm started a train of thought. There was money to be made due to a revival in demand for the product and the development of new methods of extraction. But, alas, I had no foreshore right. A few enquiries established that the 'Holmie Boys' of former years were wont to enter into an agreement with one of the syndicate which owned the Holm, pledging themselves to work for a year on his farm without pay in exchange for bed and board, the freedom of the Holm and all its "facilities", and a supply of food and other necessities when it was necessary to become resident offshore. It was a two-way act of faith. The Holm might fail to produce a worthwhile harvest, and, on the other hand, the sponsoring farmer might get the worst of the bargain should there prove to be almost constant kelp-making.

I knew John Stevenson of Rusland, and my first overtures were well received. I had the reputation of being a "good hand", and, in addition I was a passable amateur blacksmith and farrier, a valuable asset on any farm. He went so far as to suggest that, even if the venture was not an unqualified success, he "would see that I didn't lose by it". He even offered me the use of his boat! But I had no crew! However, help was at hand. At the farm of Benziecott there were a father and three able-bodied sons, and the father was also a shareholder in the Holm. There was more man-power than the farm could absorb. More overtures, a little persuasion, and perhaps a little infectious enthusiasm, and I had a crew! Danny, a great gentle giant of a man, and his youngest brother, Jim, still a youth but tall and strong, were willing to join me in what was regarded in some circles as a harebrained escapade. The fact that Danny had a skiff of his own, and was an excellent seaman, was an unexpected and valuable bonus.

The bargain having been struck, and I being free, no time was wasted! There was no question of waiting for the official farm 'term'. There was plenty of work at Rusland, with the harvest coming on. I was duly provided with a horse and cart to move my 'kist' to Rusland, and operation 'Holmie' came one step nearer. While we made tentative preparations for our expedition and waited for the storms that would tear the tangles from their anchorages there was plenty to be done on the farm. There was ploughing (with a pair of horses in those days) and cattle to be fed, oats to be threshed, together with the hundred and one jobs which according to Parkinson's Law proliferate to occupy the man-power available. On wet days we occupied ourselves largely in the time-honoured task of 'windin' simmons' in preparation for the final 'tekin' oot' of the oat stacks for the winter. It was a quiet and congenial occupation;

the barn was warm; conversation flowed. Sometimes a neighbour would look in and, in the old Westray way, he would sit down and add his quota to the clew.

Inevitably the conversation turned to Rusk Holm. The revival of an old custom was a matter of island interest, and many tales were recounted of the Holmie Boys of old and the dire disasters which had befallen them. Apart from having been terrified by the ghost of a long-dead Norwegian mariner, my predecessors had apparently suffered proximity to drowning, had been storm-stayed in the Holm until the catching and slaughtering of a 'Holmie' sheep had at least been contemplated if not actually executed. It was the fact that I knew most of the stories to be either apocryphal or pure invention for my benefit that kept me from getting cold feet.

Eventually, towards the end of December the first real 'ware-brak' came with a regular 'scriever fae the west', the proper airt for the Holm to receive its full quota of tangles. It was all systems go! In a couple of days, when the sea had calmed sufficiently, the 'Holmie Box', previously retrieved from the rafters of the barn, scalded, scrubbed and aired, was filled with a selection of good Rapness fare. There was a joint of 'reestit' bacon, a cabbage, a bag of oatmeal for porridge, a boiled chicken, a bundle of salt cod, a slab of butter, a cheese, sugar, salt, boiled milk - the list was limited only by the capacity of the box. The box was loaded on to the cart together with a bag of potatoes, a drum of paraffin, a keg of fresh water, cooking utensils, bedding, and a few 'winlins' of straw to relieve the boards of the holm bunks, and with old Rose between the shafts we foregathered at the noust. Danny and Jim were provided with an impressive pile of provisions as well, and by the time all was loaded into the skiff there was so little freeboard that sail was out of the question. That was before the days of marine motors, so we settled down to row the two miles with old Tammas o' Benziecott's advice and valedictions following us out of earshot.

Less than an hour's rowing brought us to the north east geo of the Holm. The remainder of the morning was spent in transporting our equipment to the 'hoose' and trying to induce some semblance of home into its bleak interior. Then, while Jim struggled with an uncooperative peat fire and a cold damp 'lum', Danny and I assessed the harvest of tangles - a very ample harvest indeed - and beached a useful pile of drift wood. Several sodden bodies of sheep testified to the violence of the storm and the fact that they had been caught on the skerry by the tide. Many are saved by the 'Fort' which is a cairn of stones upon which they can climb above the waves, but such casualties are not infrequent.

Jim was left to his fate as cook; eventually he appeared red-eyed to announce that dinner was ready. It was a modest enough beginning - salt cod, boiled together with potatoes in their skins, all in one pot, and in sea water! It was necessary to conserve our limited supply of fresh water as the Holm provided only a small pool of brackish liquid, the bathing place of hundreds of sea birds. The sea water furnished the necessary salt together with whatever minerals, beneficial or otherwise, are available in the Westray Firth. We suffered no ill effects, and we thoroughly enjoyed our meal, topped by a hunk of cold treacle duff thoughtfully provided by Jim's mother. After dinner our first task was to bring in a supply of peats to dry for future use, and to dig and stack a further quota. It is an unwritten law that when peat is used the users must replenish the stock, so that there is always a supply both in the event of shipwreck and for use during the annual 'sheepright' when flock management is carried out.

And so our career as Holmie Boys was launched. Every crevice and geo was piled full of tangles, and our objective was to secure as many as possible lest the wind should change and the next tide carry them to some other shore. At first it was back-breaking work. Each tangle was pulled from the heap, the frilly top removed lest it should set up rot during the drying stage, and the great rough thong hurled above high water mark. The most painful part, which took days of stoical endurance to overcome, was the flesh around the thumb nail. A nick with a nail was necessary to start the process of decapitation, and a sharp bend completed the process; however we developed a kind of mechanical routine, a rhythm - pull - nick - bend - throw; pull - nick - bend - throw. We learned to endure aching, raw thumbs, and the activity of movement kept our blood circulating so that we soon forgot the cold of the December sea water. By nightfall we had accumulated a very encouraging pile, and we adjourned for tea to find the atmosphere of the house pleasantly warm after the chill of the evening air. The lum had warmed, and the peat reek had found its proper path, although a fair proportion filtered into the atmosphere through gaps in the outer wall!

The smouldering peat was stirred into life, and soon the kettle sang. As soon as it boiled its place on the 'crook' was taken by a panful of eggs fried in butter, and the 'brö' soaked up in slices of fried bread. As we ate we took stock of our temporary home. There was little comfort, but the flickering fire was cheerful, and the mellow light of the oil lamp hung from the rafters served to soften the harsh outlines of the bare stone walls. I, as so-called leader of the project, was accorded the dignity of the "arm chair" - the massive oak "knee" from some long lost sailing ship; driftwood arms had been crudely nailed on and a sack filled with musty straw interposed between flesh and timber. Danny and Jim sat on a rough wooden bench facing me across the table which had sometime known the chartroom, perhaps of the same ship that had provided my "throne". We must have looked like a Rembrandt painting, half in light and half in shade. The table could not readily be moved because its equilibrium on the floor of living rock depended on its legs maintaining the precise position to which they had been adjusted.

Sleeping accommodation consisted of a two-tier wooden bunk designed to accommodate four. No interior springing here - just a liberal padding of fresh straw covered with a blanket. The wooden framework was an essay in holmie history with the names of former incumbents carved with varying degrees of skill. Some we had known, most we knew by reputation; all were dead. It says much for the isolation of Rusk Holm that the ubiquitous Kilroy had not so far joined the roll of honour.

The opposite corner beside the fireplace was occupied by a cupboard, known as 'the press', also obviously of maritime origin. The old laird who built the 'hoose' intended it primarily to be a kelp store, and worker comfort had been a secondary objective. The other end of the house was soon to be used for its original purpose, but meanwhile it held a collection of kelp rakes, hand barrows, rusty forks, and other decaying tools of a long abandoned trade, all of which would soon have to be repaired or replaced. Fence posts and wire netting were there also, stored against the summer day when the sheepright would require them to be strategically placed to contain the panicking flock driven out of their senses by a whooping shouting army of men, women and children. Through the tangle of impedimenta bits of wall showed, stained a dark silvery gray from contact with the stored kelp of bygone days. Above us the bare rafters supporting the roof of Caithness slate caught the glints of the fire and an occasional glimmer of moonlight filtering through the one skylight; apart from the east facing door there was no other ingress for daylight. However, the door was usually left open as long as possible as an essential aid to the ventilation of the erratic lum, so the absence of a window went unnoticed.

After tea, a smoke, a brief yarn, it was up and at it again. By the light of the moon we were able to stack our day's harvest of tangles. Jim, although he manfully did his stint, was disapproving. To his youthful mind the whole project was a "fun" thing rather than a serious means of livelihood. But there was never any major disagreement.

Moonlight working was the exception rather than the rule, but there were occasions when tide and weather made it imperative to harvest every available tangle. I can recall an occasion when we were working in oilskins and thigh-length boots at the edge of the tide in a rocky geo, sheltering occasionally behind an outcrop of rock when a shower of hail stung our faces. A gasp sounded behind me, and I turned to see in a fleeting gleam of moonlight the shining eyes of an inquisitive seal a few feet above me. Nature was never very far away from us on the holm, night or day.

And so the evening and the morning was the first day. We repeated such activities many times during the winter months, often before an audience of inquisitive selkies who seemed to accept us as fellow dependents on the bounty of the sea. We returned to shore at weekends as far as possible, although bad weather sometimes disrupted our plans. None of the dire tales of terror and hardship were repeated in our case, save for the one incident when we were awakened by a series of thumps and groans from the region of the door. As I slept in the upper bunk I felt relatively safe, although the hairs on the nape of my neck crawled perceptibly, and it fell to the lot of brave Danny to investigate. He found a large bull seal trying to ensconce himself against the relative warmth of the wood, and we all slept again, although it was not always easy to sleep when the wind was howling in the lum, and the roar of the sea was almost deafening. On moonlit nights when the wind drove the clouds across the moon, the light through the single skylight wove fantastic patterns across the rafters until I could fancy that some of the tales of ghosts and seal-men I had heard were not so far-fetched after all.

On one occasion only were we in any danger. As a leading member of a local amateur dramatic company it was essential that I get ashore for a dress rehearsal, but a gale from the north-east made the launching of the skiff inadvisable, to say the least. We persisted, and just as we thought all was well, a large wave caught us and dashed the boat heavily against a sunken rock. We dragged her to the beach and assessed the damage, which amounted to one strake badly splintered and leaking freely. But, ever resourceful we thought of a solution. We filled a sack with thick mud from the 'pow' and laid it over the damage, and set off once more. As I was the instigator of the "repair" it naturally fell to my lot to secure the sack in position. This I did by sitting on it. I may have been recognised as the leader ashore, but once afloat, Danny was the undisputed skipper. All was well while we sailed close-reefed on the port tack, but on the starboard tack I found myself on the low side looking up at the empty water barrel poised above my head, and suffering occasional spurts of cold sea water down my neck. My wife maintains to this day that my habit of standing with my back to the fire stems from that episode. We made a safe landfall, and, apart from being roundly scolded by our elders for our foolhardiness, all was well. The dress rehearsal was, of course, a shambles!

As the season progressed our stock of tangles grew to very satisfactory proportions, and the project promised success, providing that we had a good 'voar'.

The final act took place on a day in July when the schooner arrived and anchored off the Holm and we mustered a fleet of boats. All our friends and relatives and not a few others assembled complete with hand barrows, wheelbarrows, and strong backs. The kelp was bagged up in the sacks provided, weighed and carried to the boats which ferried our year's work to the schooner. A keg of porter maintained high spirits, and both my sponsors at Rusland and the good folk of Benziecott excelled themselves in the provision of food. I felt a little sad at the end of the day when the schooner hoisted sail and our flotilla of boats returned to Westray. It had been a good season and we were assured of a very satisfactory financial return. We made tentative plans for a repeat performance the following year, but opportunity and wandering feet took me elsewhere.

As I concluded my story, my audience began to look a little "quiet". The **Orcadia** had rounded the point of Weatherness and a north-easterly breeze had freshened enough to stir up a bit of a lift. I did not see her again until we reached Westray. There on the pier I saw a great heap of tangles waiting to be transported 'sooth' to be processed by some humming machine controlled by a man in a white coat- somewhere far away from the selkies and the 'pickie-tarnoes' and the 'baakies'. I realised sadly that Danny, Jim, and I had been part of something which no longer was and which could never be again. We were truly the last of the Holmie Boys.

The lady, now recovered, shook my hand, wished me a

good holiday, and thanked me for my story. "You should write it down and have it published," she said. "Maybe I will," I said, "one day."

'The Black and White Queyo' and 'The Last of the Holmie Boys' first appeared in the *Orkney Magazine* some years ago.